Praise for *The Art of Startup Fundraising*

"Alejandro's *The Art of Startup Fundraising* is a must read for any entrepreneur. Clear and concise, he outlines in today's startup community the steps to successfully fundraise. This is the golden era for entrepreneurs, any good idea with proof of concept can get access to money. Know your options!"

—Angelo J. Robles, Founder and CEO of Family Office Association

"One of the biggest crimes in the startup community is to watch good ideas and good teams to go unfunded because the fundraising process isn't friendly to first-time entrepreneurs. *The Art of Startup Fundraising* is Alejandro's contribution to the ecosystem that does a masterful job filling in knowledge gaps and giving entrepreneurs the best chances of raising the capital they need."

—Frank Rotman, Founding Partner at QED Investors

"*The Art of Startup Fundraising* delivers a smooth ride on the bumpy road of raising capital and starting a business. Alejandro Cremades delivers up-to-date details and a clear vision—an important guide for any entrepreneur who seeks to build and scale a business today."

—Jeanne M. Sullivan, Co-founder, StarVest Partners

"Fundraising can be an incredibly frustrating experience for startup founders because they are at a fundamental disadvantage: they know very little about the process, and investors know a lot. Luckily, Alejandro has taken the time to assemble a detailed blueprint of how it works behind the scenes that will help any founder level the playing field and navigate the process like a pro. If you are raising money for your startup, don't start without reading this book."

—Pedro Torres-Picon, Founder and Managing Director at Quotidian Ventures

"*The Art of Startup Fundraising* translates art into science. By sharing proven formulas, strategies, and case studies that work, Alejandro Cremades provides a needed service to future entrepreneurs."

—John Cohen, Managing Partner at City Light Capital

"This ought to be a reading requirement for all entrepreneurs when building a business and raising capital. This is a very well written and informative book, by a man who is a testament to dedication and creativity when confronted with the challenges of being an entrepreneur and raising capital."

—Carter Caldwell, serial entrepreneur and Principal at Cross Atlantic Capital Partners

"Alejandro is on the bleeding edge of equity crowdfunding today. When he talks about fundraising, startups listen."

—Andrew Ackerman, Managing Director at Dreamit Ventures

"Starting a company is full of ups and downs for an entrepreneur and foremost among them can be how to raise money for it. There is no magic bullet to make the process easy, but Cremades comes close in *The Art of Startup Fundraising* by at least making it intuitive and accessible."

—Weston Gaddy, Principal at Bain Capital Ventures

"Raising capital can be tough. Alejandro provides a step-by-step guidebook to all entrepreneurs that rather spend their time thinking about changing the world instead of thinking of how to raise funds."

—Tobias P. Schirmer, Managing Partner of JOIN Capital

"A superb book on fundraising. Alejandro's guidance should arm entrepreneurs with the necessary tools to close with success a meaningful round of financing."

—Ellen Weber, Executive Director at Robin Hood Ventures

"Raising money is hard. But startup founders all over the world can make it exponentially easier by educating themselves on the process of raising equity capital before they dive into it. The practical, hands-on advice from Alejandro Cremades in this book provides a solid foundation in that self-education process. Delivered in an approachable format with a key lesson to take away every few pages, *The Art of Startup Fundraising* is essential reading for entrepreneurs everywhere."

—Allen Taylor, Managing Director at Endeavor

"There are very few complete resources available to entrepreneurs today to help them navigate the world of fundraising. Alejandro Cremades does a great job of explaining and demystifying the fundraising process. *The Art of Startup Fundraising* will, without question, provide entrepreneurs with a great jump off point."

—Sid Paquette, Managing Director, OMERS Ventures

PITCHING INVESTORS,
NEGOTIATING THE DEAL,
AND EVERYTHING ELSE
ENTREPRENEURS
NEED TO KNOW

THE
ART OF
STARTUP
FUNDRAISING

ALEJANDRO CREMADES

WILEY

Cover design: Wiley

Published by John Wiley & Sons, Inc., Hoboken, New Jersey.
Published simultaneously in Canada.

For general information on our other products and services or for technical support, please contact our Customer Care Department within the United States at (800) 762-2974, outside the United States at (317) 572-3993 or fax (317) 572-4002.

Wiley also publishes its books in a variety of electronic formats. Some content that appears in print may not be available in electronic books. For more information about Wiley products, visit our web site at www.wiley.com.

Library of Congress Cataloging-in-Publication Data:

Names: Cremades, Alejandro, author.
Title: The art of startup fundraising : pitching investors, negotiating the deal, and everything else entrepreneurs need to know / Alejandro Cremades.
Description: Hoboken, New Jersey : John Wiley & Sons, Inc., [2016] | Includes index.
Identifiers: LCCN 2015048158| ISBN 9781119191834 (hardback) | ISBN 9781119191858 (ebk); ISBN 9781119191841 (ebk)
Subjects: LCSH: Venture capital. | New business enterprises–Finance. | Entrepreneurship. | BISAC: BUSINESS & ECONOMICS / Entrepreneurship.
Classification: LCC HG4751 .C78 2016 | DDC 658.15/224–dc23 LC record available at http://lccn.loc.gov/2015048158

Printed in the United States of America

10 9 8 7 6 5 4 3 2 1

*To my parents, Bernardo Cremades and Leticia Roman,
who created me, and to my wife, Tanya Prive, who pushes
me every single day to make the impossible possible.*

Contents

Foreword

MY MOM ALWAYS SAID IT was *never* a good time to have a baby, and she had 10. Whenever she told my dad, "Okay, Eddie, I'm pregnant," he would run right out and buy another bed. When I started the Corcoran Group, I grew the company the way my mom did her family. We grew from 6 to 60 salespeople in our first five years, and from 60 to 1,000 salespeople over the next 20 years, because I knew the secret to growing a business fast is to never wait until you're ready.

Every great entrepreneur I know expands long before their business is ready. It's the only formula I know for aggressive growth. It forces you to think faster and move smarter because you're always overextended and you have to pay the rent. With growth, many times additional funding is required to support the operations.

I sit in a privileged seat as a shark/investor on the Emmy-winning reality show *Shark Tank*, and each season we hear hundreds of heartfelt pitches from passionate entrepreneurs who are looking for funding. We listen to pitches for everything from the ingenious to the ridiculous, and get to put our own hard-earned money behind the concepts we believe will be big winners. Once a deal is closed, the fun part begins when I get to work one-on-one with the entrepreneur with whom I'm investing. I shepherd them from dream to execution, past all the hurdles and hard times, and if we're all a little bit lucky, on to a genuine, breakout success!

However, before I put my time, my money, and my partner's money behind any entrepreneur, I want to know everything I can about them and make sure every business I choose is a real winner. Investing in startups is a very risky business. Most of them fail, some eventually prosper, but only a few make a 20-to-1 jackpot return.

First, I'm looking for an entrepreneur with street smarts. Most of the entrepreneurs I've met don't have street smarts, and too many of them have answers that are way too smooth for me to trust. I'm trying to single out the winners with good gut reactions who are also smart enough to trust those reactions. I'm looking for entrepreneurs who can size up people quickly and motivate them, and spot opportunities where others see only obstacles. This takes not the usual book smarts, but real live street smarts.

I want to invest in the risk takers. Every great entrepreneur I've succeeded with has an unusually high tolerance for uncertainty—in fact, they're turned on by risk. Too many would-be entrepreneurs have buttoned up business plans with lots of numbers, fancy projections, and reasonable deductions. Those aren't the ones for me.

I want to put my money on entrepreneurs who know how to get back up fast after they've been kicked in the gut. They get knocked down just like us, but unlike most of us they take very little time feeling sorry for themselves. I sometimes think to be a great entrepreneur you need to have a low enough IQ so once you're knocked down you're too stupid to lay low, and instead pop back up saying "Hit me again!" I don't think you can learn resilience; it's a built-in attitude.

To me, this is what can make or break a pitch. The best entrepreneurs have faced challenges and risen above them. That resilience is what I'm looking for when I hear new ideas on the show (and in life).

I need to invest in founders who know how to communicate. I've learned that a new business goes nowhere if it doesn't have a good salesman at the helm. Somebody's got to sell the new product or service and that's the job of the founder. At the end of every interview I find myself asking, "Would I buy from this guy? Is his sales pitch irresistible?" Based on the answer to that one question, I turn down 95 percent of the businesses that are presented to me.

I've learned that the number-one rule in sales is that everybody wants what everybody wants and nobody wants what nobody wants. When you tell someone they *can't* have something, they always want it more, but let that same person know there's plenty to go around and they'll always go home to think about it. If you don't have people clamoring for your venture, you've got to dream up a way to create the illusion that there is demand. This is why salesmanship is key in fundraising.

Good salesmanship is never anything more than emphasizing the positives and playing down the negatives. And if you can find a unique gimmick, you'll have a huge leg up when raising capital, and also over your competition while you are executing on your vision.

I first learned the power of using a good gimmick as a young waitress in a New Jersey diner, trying to compete with Gloria, a blond bombshell with attention-grabbing breasts. Following my mom's advice, I tied red ribbons to my blonde pigtails to look like the innocent virgin I was. My tips immediately doubled. When I started my real estate brokerage company, the Corcoran Group, I used lots of gimmicks to build my brand.

I'm always looking for someone who's a bit arrogant, as I've learned that aggressive entrepreneurs bring home the bacon. They make lousy employees, have issues with authority, and don't want to be told what to do. I like to put my money in the hands of an entrepreneur who thinks he or she knows more than me. They'll need that kind of confidence to jump over the huge obstacles that stand between them and the finish line.

What I like best about angel investing is that I get to use everything I've already learned on *Shark Tank*. How do you impress an angel? How do you win their confidence and get their investment? There are tons of new business ideas out there—good, bad, and crazy—and I've seen my fair share of them all. The difference between a good idea and one that makes money is simple: *It's gotta make sense*. The idea can either be a totally new invention lots of people will use or a much better way of doing something that's been done a hundred times before.

Another key ingredient that I look for when investing in a new company is work ethic. Before I invest in any business, I'm looking for a partner. A fancy website may get me in the door, but if you can't woo an angel, you won't woo your customers and build a huge success.

This book by Alejandro Cremades will help entrepreneurs in obtaining a clear understanding of how fundraising works and what it takes to be successful in the process in order to impress people who invest in the startup ecosystem, like myself.

Alejandro's experience as the founder of Onevest makes this book unique, as the fundraising game has been changing substantially over the past years with the implementation of new laws that were introduced with the JOBS Act. With the capital moving into the online world very quickly, this book should be a must-read for any entrepreneur who is beginning to raise capital to build their venture.

—Barbara Corcoran
Investor on ABC's *Shark Tank*
Founder of the Corcoran Group

Acknowledgments

THIS BOOK WOULD HAVE NOT BEEN possible without the patience of my wife, Tanya Prive. At the time of writing this book she was pregnant with our first daughter. Tanya is the love of my life and without her by my side I highly doubt I would have been able to make it this far. I still remember the day I called her and said I wanted to give up my legal career to change the world. She did not hesitate for even a second about jumping on board with me on this crazy journey. We have experienced many ups and downs together. She is my better half and cannot wait for what the future holds for us.

Thank you as well to my parents, Bernardo Cremades and Leticia Roman. They have been my unconditional supporters and are always there for me when I need them the most. My father has been a great inspiration to me, as he also started his own business away from home when he was young. My mother has been concerned for me during the hard times and has always picked up the phone at 1 A.M. when I needed to talk to someone.

My brother, Bernardo Cremades Jr., has been a great sounding board as well as being my best friend. He is the godfather of my daughter. In fact he was the first investor of Onevest, before we even had PowerPoint slides. When we were young he took care of me and always looked after me, making sure that I would make the right decisions at school and outside of school. When I told him that I wanted to give up my law career and start an entrepreneurial journey, he was incredibly supportive. My sister-in-law, Beatriz Larrea, has also been amazing and understanding at all times.

Furthermore, I would like to thank my father-in-law and mother-in-law, Robert Shereck and Gisele Prive, not only for their generous support but also because they have been a very valuable asset with the work that they have kindly given our team in order to transform inside and outside the way we are, the way we think, and the way we execute via the services of their company, Legacy Transformational Consulting.

I could not forget my two brothers-in-law, Evan and Zack Prive. Evan has shown me how to get out of my comfort zone by target shooting in the deserts of Nevada. Zack interned with us over the course of 2014 and was very helpful.

Carmen Posadas has given me great advice through the process of putting together this book. Her wealth of knowledge and experience as a successful author has provided a wonderful guidance in this journey. I still remember the dinner at a restaurant in Madrid in which Carmen encouraged me to move forward with writing this book, and for that I am very thankful.

Moreover, I would like to thank all the people who have been involved with Onevest since its inception, including employees, advisors, and investors. They have been always there to provide great feedback and I am very proud of everything that we have been able to build together as a team since we started this journey back in 2011.

I would like to especially thank the Onevest team and our former colleagues: Carol Lee, Carles Capell, Shahab Kaviani, Nathaniel Cotanch, May Sun, Drew Butler, Erica Duignan, Sonny Tulyaganov, Cristian Gonzalez, Jacobo Tarragon, Ben Center, Dasha Sukovatitsyn, Jeffrey Fidelman, Brooks Swinnerton, Kasia Whiteis, Israel Villanueva, Tiffany Tam, Mike Hughes, Cena Crane, Lisa

Lovallo, Jonathan Block, Greg Kuwaye, Michael Whitehouse, Tim Houghten, Kammy Wood, and Culin Tate.

Thank you Barry Shereck, for being a rockstar CFO and for spending countless hours and weekends figuring out "where the bacon is" from a business perspective. You have been truly a gift and a great addition to the board and the team. I will forever treasure those long weekends that we spent at your house figuring things out.

Last but not least, I would like to acknowledge Onevest's board members: Ted Vucurevich, Javier Santiso, and Benjamin Coppel; and our advisors: Sangeet Choudhary, Anyndya Ghoose, and Barbara Corcoran. They have played a critical role in making Onevest what it is today.

Thank you all. I am very privileged and lucky to have you in my life.

1

Everything Started with Onevest

WITH THE ENCOURAGEMENT OF MY PARENTS, Bernardo Cremades and Leticia Roman, I moved to the United States from Spain with my brother Bernardo on August 13, 2008, after obtaining my law degree in Spain.

My brother is without a doubt my very best friend. On that day, after picking up our luggage and getting into a taxi, we were both completely wowed as we gazed through the windows on our way to Manhattan from the airport, while the driver, Luigi, told us his life story with a thick Italian accent.

Initially, the plan was for me to earn my masters in International Business and Trade Law at Fordham Law School and then practice law as an attorney. I had a great time at Fordham, even though some of my classmates were old enough to be my parents. They all called me Junior.

Three months before my graduation from Fordham, I received a great offer from the respected law firm King & Spalding. The partner who hired me was Edward Kehoe. Our first meeting was over breakfast at the Metropolitan Club. Ed is now a good friend, and he attended my wedding.

I still remember my first day at the firm. It was like a Hollywood movie. At only 23 years old, I had my own secretary and my name on the entrance to my own office. It was completely surreal.

After three years at King & Spalding representing major corporations in high-profile, billion-dollar investment arbitration cases, I discovered my true calling. It all started when I attended my first New York Tech Meetup with my good friend Luis Jose Scull. At the time, Luis was working for a hedge fund and sourcing tech startups as investors.

One thing really surprised me as I immersed myself in the New York tech scene, and that was how difficult it was for entrepreneurs to access capital. When I researched cases like Pandora (rejected over 300 times before securing their first significant round of financing), I knew there was a big gap in the market. There was something missing and I wanted to find out what it was and fill that gap.

At the time of this discovery phase, I was dating the woman who is now my wife, Tanya Prive. Choosing her as my life partner is the best decision I have ever made. We talked about what I wanted to do to help others looking for capital, and I convinced her to invest all our savings in Onevest and launch a platform that would connect entrepreneurs with investors, and from that point on, the rest was history.

Everything started at Tanya's apartment on 27th Street and 6th Avenue in New York City. We had a little studio where we would invite at least five interns a day to join us in building the product, and they worked with a team of engineers that we had assembled in Belarus (Eastern Europe). After four months of interns claiming they were our cousins, the building management figured out that something was up and invited us to leave.

We then rented an office space, raised a seed round, and started to hire top talent. After one year of development, we were able to launch the platform to the public on November 23, 2011. A few months later, the platform was mentioned by *TIME* as one of the best crowdfunding platforms in the world. It was listed as one of the top-10 digital tools for entrepreneurs by *Forbes*, and we were named one of the hottest startups to watch by *Business Insider*. I also had the honor of being ranked number one on *Vanity Fair's* list of "30 under 30" for 2014, and I was included on the "Top 30 under 30" list in *Entrepreneur Magazine* (Spanish version).

The press attention was crazy to me, but what kept me moving was the opportunity to make a real difference. Cutting the noise is one of the hardest things that entrepreneurs have to master in order to focus on what really counts, which is the execution of business strategy.

In the early days it was not easy. We had to fight to provide financing. The JOBS Act (which we will discuss later on in this book) was still not in the picture, and the word *crowdfunding* had not yet been coined. At one point in the process we visited the White House and testified before the U.S. House of Representatives regarding the importance of financing small businesses in the United States.

Everything started to happen at the same time. To our surprise, we were suddenly riding an amazing wave, forming with the passing of the JOBS Act in April of 2012. For the first time in history startups would be allowed to advertise the fact that they were raising money; before the JOBS Act this kind of promotion was completely forbidden. (Prior to that legislation, it was labeled as general solicitation.) Previously, the search for funds was more a word-of-mouth kind of activity. If you did not know anyone in Silicon Valley, it was a real struggle to find capital.

At the end of 2013, a company called CoFoundersLab.com came to raise financing on Onevest, and lit up a light bulb in my mind. I realized that a fundraising platform like the one that Onevest was operating at that moment was really playing a small game. The bigger game was to build an ecosystem around Onevest, where we would empower entrepreneurs and investors, from formation to financing.

As a result of that realization, the conversations began with Shahab Kaviani, the cofounder of CoFoundersLab.com, and we ended up announcing an M&A transaction to bring CoFoundersLab under Onevest in July 2014.

Currently, CoFoundersLab is the largest matchmaking service for entrepreneurs. It's a way for entrepreneurs to meet their cofounders and advisors. We are partners with some of the major startup hubs in America, and we are onboarding thousands of entrepreneur registrations on a monthly basis.

Other products under the umbrella of Onevest include, most recently, 1000 Angels, which is the first digital, invitation-only network for a select group of angel investors. It is a curated community of ultra high-net-worth individuals that come together to invest in startup companies.

After seeing hundreds of businesses formed and financed through the ecosystem of Onevest, I felt it was time to share what I'd learned and help entrepreneurs on their journeys in fundraising—especially after our most recent round of financing, in which we'd increased our total amount raised to over $5 million. We self-crowdfunded our Series A in a matter of weeks and established a record. I literally did not move from my desk. The result was a huge surprise, as these types of rounds would have normally meant spending at least eight months out of the office, attending conferences and meetings to gather investor interest.

Unfortunately the company announcements of successfully closed rounds of financing that you see and hear about are not the reality. They come from only a few companies out of the many, many ventures that launch each year. Raising capital is an art. Every single ingredient needs to be perfectly balanced in the process in order to secure capital successfully. This book aims to be the guide that will help you get there in a process that, many times, can be a rollercoaster ride, full of emotions.

Fasten your seat belt and embrace the process. Be optimistic and have fun with it. Remember, you will never fail—you will either succeed or learn.

2

Raising Capital for Your Startup

BEFORE RUSHING INTO PREPARING PITCHING materials, meeting investors, and hammering out funding terms, it is critical to get your mindset, expectations, math, and strategy right.

Speeding Up the Machine

Some opportunists and entrepreneurs see the promise of funding or financing as the chance to get someone else to put money on the line to build their dream into reality, especially when it is a product or tool that can only be brought to life with major money. (Space exploration and revolutionary health-care progress are great examples of this.) But these types of fundraising missions represent big risks for investors. And if you've tried walking into a bank for a startup loan, you already know that it's going to be a challenge.

There is another way to approach raising capital for your startup. It's meant to speed up the machine, not build it. This can really present the best opportunity for both fundraisers and funders. By building the product first, entrepreneurs establish that ownership, control, and lead. They also have the opportunity to build and hone a business model that works regardless of additional funds. That's a much more powerful fundraising and negotiating position to be in. On the other side of the table investors are able to put their money to work with confidence, in a startup that has a product, and one which is proven to work. More money just helps to speed up the achievement of various milestones, and to magnify the successes and strengths.

When you are raising money from outsiders, there will be expectations to deliver certain types of milestones in a given timeline. For that reason, it not only helps to have a product on the market with some historical data when negotiating your financing terms, it also helps to avoid a significant dilution that comes with raising money as you're working to figure things out, assembling the machine.

Most startups eventually pivot to adjust to what the market is telling them. I have yet to see a bulletproof business plan, so it's important to have proof of concept and validation before taking the risk of bringing outsiders into the mix.

Take a moment to think and reclarify why you are raising capital. Consider what it will do for you, and what the opportunity offers to potential investors.

It's Not as Easy as Reading an Article on TechCrunch

If people read the weekly headlines on TechCrunch or various startup and fundraising blogs, it sounds as if anyone who can fog up a mirror can land several seven-figure-plus rounds of funding. Some people have the impression that if you throw up a crowdfunding page, you can land a million dollars to play with as you like. This is one of the biggest pitfalls facing startups today. It's not that easy—at least not for most startups. The truth is that it takes work. It takes effort, time, and an investment in thinking and taking the small actions that can create big results. Aside from the right mindset and expectations, successful fundraising takes making connections, marketing, and proving yourself and the product. It takes strategically rolling out and executing a plan. Often, that requires help.

According to data from Forbes and the SBA (Small Business Administration), venture capitalists fund only about 2 percent of the opportunities they review.[1] While not all new businesses need or seek funding, consider that there are around 600,000 new business entities that file each year. In the first quarter of 2012, only 3 percent of venture capital (VC) funds went to brand-new startups, while 97 percent went to ventures that were already running. This information is not to discourage you from your startup, or from raising capital, but rather it is meant to better prepare you for what you need to do to effectively and efficiently score the capital you want. While it's important to build the product first, whenever possible, and prove the concept, you can choose to create a starter version, or MVP (minimum viable product), or provide other proof of testing and demand. Define what makes you convinced that this venture is a go, and that it is a good opportunity for investors.

The 18- to 24-Month Plan

The savviest founders give themselves plenty of time and cushion to raise the capital they are aiming for, and 18 to 24 months is a good timeframe.

Don't worry, this doesn't mean putting everything else on pause, or slowing down your startup. In fact, continuing to clock progress in development, branding, your client base, and sales can help in the fundraising process.

Perhaps you already have a business plan, and have even started selling and building great relationships and establishing distribution channels. That's fantastic. But you will need to meld your business plan and your fundraising plan together, if they aren't already a part of the same document. Perhaps you initially thought you wouldn't

[1] http://www.forbes.com/sites/dileeprao/2013/07/22/why-99-95-of-entrepreneurs-should-stop-wasting-time-seeking-venture-capital/#48398d84296d.

need outside funding, but now you see the advantages, or you thought you could land a bank loan, but it didn't happen. Or, you are just now realizing that raising substantial amounts of capital in the best way is going to take a little longer than you think. Just take the time to recalibrate and ensure synergy as you progress.

Whatever your number is, break it down by funding rounds and by business milestones. Divide your needs into easily actionable steps that will take you where you want to go in the next 18 to 24 months.

Milestones

Notable milestones to be achieved during your startup and fund-raising process include:

- Idea conceptualization
- Market research
- Business plan creation
- Testing the waters
- Finding your cofounders
- Making key hires
- Building a board
- Prototypes and beta testing
- Launch of a minimum viable product
- Expanding early adopters and users
- Gaining revenues
- Proof of demand and potential for scale
- Breakeven point

Entrepreneurs should be focused on raising the capital to make it to the next milestone and round of funding. This amount should include a cushion for overages, and a budget for marketing for more funds. Work toward each milestone and give it the proper attention, even if you have the long goal of an IPO, buyout, or putting a legacy business on autopilot.

Breaking Even

While there are many milestones in the process of launching, nurturing, and growing a startup, the breakeven point cannot be overlooked. Let's be honest—until the breakeven point is reached, all income is burned cash. (And that even applies when the numbers are in the tens of billions of dollars.) But once the breakeven point is reached, startup founders can then negotiate from a place of power, and they technically don't need another outside dollar. However, additional funding can certainly help. That money can be funneled into real growth, and maximized.

It is important to note that many of the biggest companies, and those that have attracted major investment, still haven't achieved the breakeven point. It isn't a prerequisite for raising capital. Peter Thiel tackles this issue in his book *Zero to One*. He reminds us that the real value of a company, and how savvy investors view opportunities, is the future value of cash flow. If you aren't breaking even today, when will you be? How much future cash flow can investors buy into? What discount are they getting by buying into that cash flow now?

Expectations of Investors

What are the expectations of investors? Unless startups know what investors expect and are looking for, it's hard to give the right signals, prepare, and position your company to be the recipient of funding. So what do investors really want? In asking this question, it's often easiest to first address what they don't want, which is:

- To lose money
- To be made to look foolish

Everything else, including expectations, circles back to avoiding these two pain points. Some expectations may be arrived at naturally and individually. Many others are line items that investors believe they need to check off. But they all come back to avoiding these pain points. Here is a list of the 19 items that investors want and expect:

1. A well-thought-out and researched business idea and plan
2. Organization
3. Integrity and character
4. Answers to obvious questions
5. That you know what you don't know and don't have, but you have a plan to get it
6. Market potential
7. Plans for repayment if seeking a loan
8. Plans for additional rounds of funding and/or exits
9. That you have put your heart into the project
10. That you have and will keep skin in the game
11. Feedback from others
12. Proof of demand
13. That they can get along with you
14. That you are coachable
15. Consideration of the safety of their capital and time
16. A good match
17. Passion for your product or service
18. Passion for connecting with and working with them
19. An opportunity that will take them closer to their goals

While pitching and engaging in other fundraising efforts (and even in the activities leading up to those efforts), entrepreneurs must keep in mind that they are not selling their product. They are selling an investment in their company. This shouldn't mean completely redesigning the venture and sacrificing the original vision simply to raise funding (although some do go through the process when it becomes apparent that it is needed).

Still, if founders work to know their investors as they do their customers, they'll find the fundraising process easier. Understand investors' fears and pain points, their checkboxes, and their goals. This doesn't just mean cold monetary goals. Go well beyond promised ROI and crude sales and cash-flow predictions. Institutional and individual investors have metrics and numbers that they are trying to hit.

What else drives investors to invest? Outdoing their competition, bragging rights, strategic navigating, the desire for security, and a drive to fulfill their potential fuels and facilitates solutions that they care about. These are constants. Then there are the factors that are more spontaneous and heat of the moment. Does a decision maker need to impress or please someone else in the chain by making an investment? Can a *Shark Tank* scenario be created that fuels competition between investors?

As much as we each believe otherwise, when we launch a venture, a startup is far from a sure thing. Without capital and connections and expertise that can influence markets' future performance, a startup is often a string of optimistically strung-together dots and assumptions. Refer to the checklists in this chapter often to give yourself an advantage.

Outperform the Competition

One of the best ways to attract capital is to outperform the competition. This will certainly help in your pitches, presentations, and discussions, all while boosting results and your negotiating strength. And it might just help you get noticed and draw attention, minimizing the work and investment involved in chasing money.

There are different measures of outperforming. Can you outperform in profit margin, sales, social media, startup battles, or growth? How about outperforming on fundraising? Peter Thiel points out that Twitter is a great example of this. While Twitter might have a lot of work to do, it has shown great growth versus a declining print news industry.

Outperforming in growth means people believe in future potential, and indicates there is a time to get in while there is still a perceived discount available. So, find your edge, and define a metric that you can outperform on.

If you are not already outperforming on one of these metrics or need to create more distance ahead of the competition, pick your strong suit and lean in. Don't unnaturally force something that will derail the venture, or sabotage your fundraising potential. Look for an edge you can hone and maximize.

So how do you gain traction or visibility in this area when you are already going all out? Eight methods are recommended.

1. Prioritize and focus attention on that area
2. Get help
3. Get up earlier
4. Compete in competitions
5. Participate in development or coding marathons
6. Attend conferences
7. Go to networking sessions
8. Join invitation-only communities of like-minded people

Marketing

The majority of startups have to market themselves to have any hope of getting funding. They have to market hard, and outmarket hundreds of thousands of competing startups and existing businesses. Do not underestimate the time and money investment required for marketing—both ongoing and fundraising-specific marketing. All marketing speaks to potential investors. It tells them a story about the value and potential of your company, and what you are really about.

Done right, your regular marketing can go a long way in helping to position your startup to attract and convert investors—especially angel investors. If initial marketing and branding is done with fundraising in mind, results can be maximized, and your budget can go further. So look for crossover potential, and review messaging with fundraising in mind.

Your initial marketing may include branding materials, websites, and other online assets, apps, rounds of testing, sponsorships, product placement, social media, in-person networking, and more.

Don't burn out on marketing. Don't burn up your marketing budget and bankrupt your startup and fundraising mission right before you see results. Plan to need to market longer than you think until you secure funding and see your cash replenished.

Don't take the excitement or early investor advantage out. Make sure messaging has seamless synergy with your pitch-deck messaging, and your presentation. Ask "Is this going to appeal to, turn on, and compel our target investors to write a check on the spot? Or will it send them running and telling their investor friends to stay away?"

Note that investors will be more interested in organic growth. This means building channels that give you traffic without having to invest capital in order to acquire users. This could mean crushing it on search engines, or a serious viral loop on your product that keeps bringing people in the door. Venture capital firms are enthusiastic about social networking effect. They go crazy when they see the entrepreneur has figured out how to crack that code.

Storytelling

Storytelling is a critical part of marketing for startups. It's a critical part of marketing, branding, building consumer loyalty, and growth for fledgling startups and the largest international corporations alike. For startups, it can be the make-or-break part of the pitch. It also has a place in the elevator pitch, pitch deck, verbal branding, visual branding, website content, and perhaps even in your tagline.

Businesses that have blossomed through storytelling include TOMS, Patagonia, and the Dollar Shave Club.[2] Every brand and venture has a story. Even if you don't realize it, you have a story, and it is what has led you to where you are today. Everyone has a unique story, and different brands leverage different parts of their stories to

[2] www.referralcandy.com/blog/storytelling-in-marketing-11-examples/.

reach their goals. Zappos's story was all about company culture. Airbnb's has largely been about the "sharing economy" movement. Apple's is about Steve Jobs. Fast growing nonprofit Acumen has done an incredible job of incorporating masses of supporters in its story with books, interactive classes, volunteer chapters, and Google+ community groups.

Ultimately, the best entrepreneurs are not the best visionaries. The greatest entrepreneurs are incredible salespeople. They know how to tell an amazing story that will convince talent and investors to join in on the journey.

Many entrepreneurs unfortunately overlook the value and importance of storytelling, and focus on technical info, which investors and consumers simply can't relate to. It doesn't matter how great your invention or innovation is if people can't relate, and if you can't speak their language.

Even if you don't plan to purposefully use storytelling, or don't particularly like your version of your story, document it. Document everything that led up to the idea. Document every step of the journey. You have a story. If you don't tell the story, others will make up a story about you and your business or product in their minds, and it might not be the story that serves you best. By documenting your story, you can look back and pick out the best parts of it, or have an expert and friends review and highlight what they believe the strongest parts of your story are. Sometimes you are too close to your story. A professional storyteller and branding expert can objectively leverage the most powerful elements of your story for the overall mission.

Daily journaling is a common habit of highly successful entrepreneurs, and if you haven't started, this is the opportune time to begin. Journaling can help you connect the dots regarding how life has prepared you and carried you to this point, what drove you to make this leap, what is unique about your process, and what is better about your product or service. This can all facilitate deep connections with potential investors. And the story will develop over time as your venture evolves. It may begin with you or a specific customer profile, and then unfold into a story about the journey and a far wider population.

If you'd like to get better at storytelling, or are searching for ideas and pieces to your storytelling puzzle, check out author Seth Godin's books and blog, and see digital storyteller Amanda Lewan's post "Storytellers: 100 Ways to Spark Inspiration."[3]

Some of the best entrepreneurs are those who are highly articulate in telling their story and describing the problem they are resolving through their startup and the reason why they started.

I was once on a panel judging a startup competition. The startup that won was creating the Uber for psychologists. She explained how she had been inspired to start the company as a result of a mental illness in her family, and her story nearly brought the crowd to tears.

Leveraging Help

If storytelling isn't your area of expertise, don't be shy about getting some help. The same applies to business planning, a fundraising plan, creating a pitch deck, verbal and visual branding, PR, and even negotiating funding terms.

Truly wise entrepreneurs are those who are smart enough to know what they don't know, and when to leverage an expert. There are many ways to do this, and options that can fit even into the shoestring budgets of young startups. These ways include:

- Friends and family that are experienced professionals
- Trusted existing mentors
- Members of your own "mastermind group"
- Professionals and businesses offering workshops and free advice sessions
- Cofounders
- Volunteers and interns
- Freelancers

---

[3] www.amandalewan.com/blog/inspiration/7-storytellers-100-ways-to-spark-inspiration.

- Existing investors
- Advisors
- Former colleagues
- CoFoundersLab's network of advisors and cofounders

You might be surprised who can help if you ask. Just make sure you are getting quality advice. If you are able to leverage free help and advice, be respectful of people's time and look for ways to give back and add value.

I love the United States because it is a country where you can pick up the phone and call anyone, or send an email to anyone. This is something that does not happen in other cultures, such as Spain, where I come from. Remember, there is nothing to lose. Ask! People truly live by the pay-it-forward philosophy.

If you can't find enough volunteers locally, then freelancers and on-demand outsourced team members can be an excellent resource. In fact, you'll find that this kind of outsourcing is a common go-to for hot Silicon Valley startups and booming businesses that make the Inc. 500 list of the fastest-growing private companies.

There are now multiple platforms for finding and recruiting great outsourced help. However, Upwork (the merger of the two largest online freelancing platforms, oDesk and Elance) really stands out as a top choice. There, startups and entrepreneurs can find thousands of highly qualified and affordable professionals in all types of functions. You'll find copywriters, strategists, social media marketers, graphic designers, researchers, and data entry staff. Upwork makes it easy to post gigs, screen potential assistants, hire them, monitor progress, and handle bookkeeping, all in a highly efficient and streamlined way.

Divide and Conquer

Another option is to have one cofounder focus on the fundraising efforts, and all that falls underneath this. In some cases, startups will already have a founder specializing in finance and marketing. Some don't. Obviously, having a cofounder who is a master of this area of business, and whose efforts won't eat up working capital, can be a huge advantage.

If you don't have a cofounder with fundraising expertise, it may be worth looking for one. CoFoundersLab[4] can be an excellent resource for connecting with potential cofounders. If you are currently a one-founder startup, it is worth noting that investors normally prefer multifounder startups. Investors are likely to think that you are alone because you were not able to convince anyone else of the potential of your idea.

Just be wary of bringing on too many people and creating an even bigger issue with too much dilution, and complex and fragile ownership situations. More than four founders is dangerous due to an excess of opinions.

Whatever the situation, things can go far more smoothly if one person is in charge of the fundraising initiative. Pick someone. Let that person own it.

The Rollercoaster of Emotions

Let's be clear about one thing—no matter how great the planning, the adventure of launching a startup and raising capital is going to be an emotional journey.

No matter how professional, cool, and businesslike you are, it is going to be tough—that is, unless you don't really care about the venture that much, in which case you may as well just stop here.

If you do care, and if you are truly burning with passion to make your vision a reality, know that through the highs of launching, breaking through major milestones, and landing substantial funding, there are going to be some ups, downs, and curves to navigate. So hold on tight.

The experience doesn't have to mean taking an emotional beating if you have realistic expectations. Choose in advance

---

[4] https://www.cofounderslab.com/.

how you are going to deal with issues and surprises. You can get to your goal, but even the brightest and most connected can struggle to acquire funding.

Consider LawPivot, "the 99 designs for legal services." The startup was founded by Silicon Valley lawyers Nitin Gupta and Jay Mandal (Apple's leading M&A lawyer) and received over $1.6 million in seed funding, including backing from Google Ventures. The business was later bought by Rocket Lawyer, which has $20 million in annual revenues. In spite of all this, the business wasn't an overnight success.[5] Getting to success took tweaking the pitch, plenty of emails, and time.

Expect fundraising to take longer than you expect. Be ready for some unexpected feedback. Be prepared to make some pivots and adjustments, to hurry up and wait, to be disappointed and frustrated—and be sure to have patience. In the long term, it is all so worth it! If you are mentally prepared, the rollercoaster ride won't be too severe and you'll be far more likely to succeed. Most entrepreneurs give up only a few minutes too soon.

Learn to Love Rejection

Learning to embrace and savor rejection is one of the best things that entrepreneurs can do. It doesn't come naturally to most adults. For kids, it's a different story. They'll happily and energetically keep on asking for that toy until their parents cave in. Launching a startup is the time to find your ever-optimistic inner child again.

If you've ever worked in sales, you may have an advantage. Mortgage and real estate pros, for example, are trained to embrace rejection from day one. They are taught that "nine nos lead to one yes." Every no means they are getting closer to that yes, that sale, that capital.

---

[5] http://techcrunch.com/2013/01/14/rocket-lawyer-acquires-lawpivot-to-add-a-quora-like-qa-platform-to-online-legal-services-site/.

Sometimes this may mean 100 nos or voicemails before hitting 10 yeses back-to-back. But you've got to keep going. Learn this concept and it will serve you well in every stage of growing your business.

The mistake that many entrepreneurs make is hearing and internalizing the word "no" from a potential investor after the first few exchanges. When you hear a no in the form of *you are too early, not enough traction*, and so forth, this basically means that you need to keep the investor updated. If you execute and deliver on what you promised in your communications, I assure you that the investor will end up investing. Keep people in the loop of your milestones and accomplishments.

Imagine if J.K. Rowling had given up after the rejections she received for her Harry Potter manuscript. What if, instead of his business taking off when he was 65 years old, after sleeping in his car while traveling and pitching his now-famous chicken with the hopes of launching a franchise, Colonel Sanders had given up at "no"? What if Abraham Lincoln hadn't pushed on after eight election failures to change history as he did? And what if Steve Jobs hadn't been so adamant about perfection?

Rejection will happen. Learn from it. Adapt. Build up immunity to it.

Connect the Dots

The dots may connect. But it is the artist (entrepreneur) who must pick up the pen and make the connections, and make the hidden picture a reality. This often begins with learning to handle rejection objectively. When it comes to seeking

> *Believing that the dots will connect down the road will give you the confidence to follow your heart.*
>
> —Steve Jobs

capital a "no" doesn't always have to stay a no. Sometimes those controlling the flow of capital just aren't hearing you right. Sometimes they need you to better connect the dots for them. Other times it is simply about timing. So don't let your emotions run away with you and cause you to burn valuable bridges. Be kind. Be open to and accept all types of feedback.

It won't always be a great match. You might not understand that in the moment, but try to gauge and learn to pinpoint when a rejection is actually a positive thing (perhaps it is a "maybe" waiting to become a "yes" if you make the right moves). Sometimes investors will simply be testing you to see how you handle rejection and if you have what it takes to stick it out. Will you pass that test? Will you persevere and follow up?

Sometimes you may need to work to connect the dots over time. If contacts with angel investors, VCs, and other contacts don't directly turn into funding, then they may at least lead to great referrals, contacts, and sales. Never leave a meeting without another introduction or another referral. Your time is your most valuable resource and you need to extract as much value as possible from it.

Remember that the most precious and priceless assets you can gain as a founder are contacts and people's attention. So don't burn trust. Find ways to stay in touch, stay in their minds, build relationships, and add value. A great way to do this is via email, through social media, and by sending snail mail (and meeting in person works, too).

So what do you say? A great example is when you met an investor, but for whatever reason they didn't bite at the opportunity at that moment. Perhaps the timing was bad for their liquidity, or they just weren't convinced by you or confident about the venture (yet). In response, you could put aside that contact and talk badly about them on Twitter. Or you can preserve and nurture that lead and relationship. What if you began a steady, passive, drip "campaign" by email, instead of reacting to that first meeting?

This might start with a thank-you email. *"Thank you for your time. I'm sorry you didn't feel you could participate in [this venture opportunity] at this time. You mentioned you were more interested in health-care startups, so here are the email addresses or links to pitch decks for three healthcare startups that are operating out of the same coworking space. Hopefully this will add some value for you."*

Or perhaps you could write: *"Thanks for your time. Just as a thank-you, here is a $50 gift card so that you can make up the time you invested with me to take your spouse out for an artisanal coffee, or to this awesome ramen restaurant I recently discovered."*

Taking time for gestures like these should certainly earn you some respect, a place in the investor's memory, and the privilege of getting your next message opened.

Maybe 90 days later, you send a second email. This time you write: *"Since you took the time to talk to me and offer your advice, I thought I'd fill you in on our progress. We've now [finished development/ have gained X amount more users/have landed seed funding from someone else]. As a second thanks, I'd love to give you or someone you know the chance to beta test our next improvement. Here's your login code. . . . "*

The third message might be: *"Great news! We are just two weeks away from hitting our next big milestone!"*

Or, *"On your advice, we brought in another cofounder that specializes in this area. Here's an updated version of our pitch deck in case you know of any other investors looking for a great opportunity right now."*

Or how about: *"Thanks again for the great advice. Our launch party is coming up next month. Here are a couple tickets as a show of appreciation. We'd love to invite you to come along and bring a guest."*

How do you think this might help you stand out, change the dynamics of the relationship, and attract opportunities for the future?

I would also like to point out that raising money is all about building relationships first—the capital comes later. Like the saying goes, "Ask for money, get advice. Ask for advice, get money twice."

The Pros and Cons of Raising Capital

Before we get any further, it is critical that you and any partners you have truly understand the pros and cons of raising capital for your startup.

The Pros of Raising Capital	The Cons of Raising Capital
More money can amplify success	Fundraising can be costly and time consuming
Leveraging power contacts and influencers	Giving up control
Speeding up results	The burden of owing others
Capital can be critical for staying afloat	Too much money destroys founders, relationships
Funds to use to improve product/service	Pressure to water down or detour from plans
Branding and visibility benefits	Can become distracted by additional demands
You can grow a lot bigger, a lot faster	You'll be pocketing less of the profits

These pros and cons are just examples. And these factors will vary depending on where you get your funding. But it's important to be aware of them: Founders must be prepared, know what their priorities are, and know what they are willing to give up and sacrifice in exchange for positive results.

Don't Underestimate the Need for Capital

No startup founder should ever underestimate the importance of access to capital. Nothing will kill your venture and dream faster than running out of cash. When you are out of cash, you can't market, promote, or get sales. You may not be able to pay vendors and staff. The consequences can go far beyond simply crashing your startup.

This isn't an issue only for brand new businesses, either. It is often the unexpected cash flow crunch later on that sabotages very promising ventures. You can have $1 billion in revenues and still be losing money.

In 2015 the Treasury Department reported that the federal government had brought in a record almost $3 trillion in only 10 months. Yet the government was still short almost $500 billion in operating money. And we've all seen the fiascos that can occur with repeated stalemates and even shutdowns. It's the same thing that got the biggest and oldest financial firms in trouble when the credit crisis hit. The biggest banks in the world and the biggest automakers had to be bailed out. So don't fool yourself into thinking you are immune. Even as this book was being written, Elon Musk's Tesla was raising an additional $500 million to prevent a cash shortage . . . and this is during good economic times.

So even if you don't think you'll need or want cash yet, having everything lined up to raise capital, or at least having substantial lines of credit turned on, can be crucial to survival. Stay strong and stay liquid. You should be raising capital 24/7. Sometimes you'll be more active, sometimes less. In any case, plan to open your round at least six months before running out of funds.

3

Setting Yourself Up for Success

BUSINESS SUCCESS REQUIRES BUSINESS PREPARATION. You don't have to be a master tactician, but you do need to have a plan in place. This plan will act as a foundation for everything you want to achieve.

Diligence is a key word in the business world for a reason. When a potential investor sees that your startup is well-thought-out and managed with a high level of expertise, with defined and realistic goals, that investor will know that your business is a solid proposition, and, therefore, the business will attract more investment. This approach is about cultivating a working process that leads to success: success for you, your startup, your investors, and your employees.

Investors Don't Want to Invest

As a startup founder, you need to understand how truly difficult it is to attract investment. Many rookie founders make the mistake of assuming that their product/service concept is so attractive that all they need to do is put the word out and watch the capital roll in. Nothing could be further from the truth.

Even with a fantastic idea, investors will still be wary. Why? Because they know that any investment could potentially fail, costing them the assets or capital they've supplied. You need to therefore begin your search for investors with one mantra: *Investors don't want to invest*. When you understand this and put it at the heart of any pitch, all of your efforts will be focused on persuading investors away from this negative outlook, and encouraging them to be part of your business.

Don't make it easy for an investor to turn down the opportunity. The investor has to want it, and he or she has to feel that an amazing business is waiting, one that could provide them substantial revenue. It is all about creating the feeling of a train that is leaving the station: if they feel the train will be waiting there forever, they will never get on board.

The Core of Your Business

Ideas are meaningless without a masterful execution. Attracting investors is about more than a great idea. It's about showing the correct preparatory skills that will persuade potential investors that you will handle their capital diligently. The most effective way to do this is to put the core structure of your business in place *before* you begin seeking substantial investment. If you have not taken the steps to prepare your business adequately, this will count against you significantly during negotiations.

There is one caveat to this, however, which is that, in some cases, you will need to seek angel investment before you can put all aspects of your core business in place. In these situations you must do what you can. This is not a license to avoid doing the work. You will still need to have adequately researched your product/service, the costs, the current marketplace, and so on in order to attract an angel investor.

There are many benefits to having your business structured, in order, and built with thought and care from the ground up. Beyond attracting investment, this process will help you cultivate a business ethos and work ethic that, when applied to all future business decisions, will significantly boost the efficiency and success of your organization.

Experienced and Talented Management

Every investor wants to know that the person in charge of their money is talented, and someone who can generate positive returns. The running of a business therefore can be boiled down to two words: *good management.*

No matter the area or industry, you'll need a comprehensive, talented, and experienced management team in place. If your startup has a strong team, then any investor can be more confident about the direction and potential of a business.

Just as Jim Collins states in his book *Good to Great*, as long as you have the right people on the right seats of the bus you will end up finding your direction. Startups need to identify a repeatable and scalable model. Investors do not expect you to have all the answers, but they at least expect that you'll have people around you who will help to you find them.

First, you will need to assess how much you personally can contribute toward management. It may be that you are fully qualified and have all the relevant experience and knowledge, but more often than not the first step a startup founder should take is to identify his or her own limitations. By bringing in managers who can perform specific tasks better, you will free yourself up to oversee other aspects of the business, knowing that operations are well in hand.

Your management team should have domain experience. A potential investor is bound to research the work history and achievements of those making key decisions within your startup. If, for example, your startup is based in the smartphone industry, and yet your management team comes from the food industry, this will not instill confidence in the investor. They want to know that the team making important decisions has done this work before, and that they know how to achieve success within your specific industry.

I am a big believer in hiring people who are smarter than you, and whom you can trust with getting the work done. At a management level you need people who can contribute a good amount of strategy to the mix.

Organize Your Corporate Structure with a Legal Team

A business is an organization—this is an important point. Your startup must be effectively organized and must have the correct corporate structure in place. Without it, your business will either suffer from poor efficiency, or end up in legal strife due to not having the correct legal documents or permits in place.

Being a recovering lawyer myself (still seeking therapy), I know how important this area is. Startups are tempted to cut corners all the time, but the legal process is not something that you want to mess with. We onboarded Peter Fusco from Lowenstein Sandler on day one. He has been fantastic to work with and the decision has given us peace of mind. I've heard plenty of nightmare stories, and I would definitely advise that you get the right counsel. Don't choose cheap services or depend on your cousin the divorce lawyer, who might give you a helping hand with corporate matters during his free time.

Remember that there are certain legal responsibilities that, if not fulfilled on the part of a startup founder, can scuttle any investment deal. If you have not filed for patents, for example, then an investor will be less likely to commit. You have to ensure that what your startup is offering cannot be simply copied by someone else in terms of branding and, under certain circumstances, technology. These aspects of your startup can be protected through patent and copyright filing, which can be handled quickly by a qualified lawyer.

You should also clear any legal disputes connected with your startup as quickly as possible. If you are in a dispute over intellectual property rights, or any other part of your business, with a previous partner or other individuals, then this will be a major impediment to investment. Any such occurrence will be made apparent during the due diligence investigation an investor will carry out, so it should be dealt with swiftly so that there are no pending legal issues casting a shadow on your company.

In the disclosure schedule that you will need to provide (within your offering materials), list all the matters that might put your business at risk. Lawsuits and other legal issues need to be included here; otherwise you might find yourself in a lawsuit, courtesy of your investors, later on down the line. In the disclosure schedule you will need to be as transparent as possible. For that reason, you need to make sure that, at any point when you are seeking money, you have already resolved any troubles or concerns that might scare people off during the disclosures.

Helpful Advisors

No business is built purely in isolation. If it is a success or failure, it is because of actions taken and the available knowledge that informed its strategies. Every startup founder must have a comprehensive knowledge of the industry they are entering, but it is also important to have access to skilled individuals who have the experience to advise on relevant scenarios as they appear.

Your advisors are a sounding board, a well of knowledge that you can return to when needed. This is especially important when you are a first-time startup founder, but even the most experienced businessperson needs to have a solid network of advisors. Why? Because no one person has all the knowledge, all the answers, or all the talent. A successful business must rely on a varied supply of these key aspects. Furthermore, there will be times when you are presented with a choice, perhaps one that could define your business. In this situation, having an experienced mentor to advise you on the pros and cons of each decision is an invaluable resource.

Choosing your advisors is more difficult. You can take personal experience into account, going to those you trust most; but in business you may have to cast your net a little wider. A good advisor will be much like your management team. (They may even double as your advisors.)

Domain knowledge and experience of your chosen industry will
help, but no single advisor will have all the answers. You may have
one advisor who has expertise in advertising, another who understands an important manufacturing process, another offering advice
on tax or important relevant legislation. Whoever they are, they
should be only individuals who can genuinely contribute.

But how do you find the right advisors? Many of them will work at
other companies, in various positions. In some instances you may be
able to hire someone to fill a consultancy-based position, but often
your advisors will be helping you for free. That might not sound very
plausible, but it is more likely than you think. Your advisors will be
made up of those individuals you have networked with. When you are
dealing with a supplier, a CEO, or an advertiser, you might put a
question to them. There is no harm in simply asking for their opinion.
Often, they will happily give it. This will cut down on consultancy
fees, but it will also build a connection to other companies and
industry players, businesses, and individuals who could help take your
startup to the next level in the future, when needed.

I suggest going to CoFoundersLab and meeting some of the
advisors we have there. CoFoundersLab has thousands of advisors on
staff looking to help entrepreneurs. You may find the right match
there.

Advisors are also a good resource to get to funding. They can open
the doors to potential investors and make the right introductions.

From my point of view, you are going to have two types of advisors.
The first type is a high-profile individual who can give credibility to
your business by leveraging their name. This could be people in your
industry who give their stamp of approval to your product. The other
type of advisor is those people who have the time to invest in your
business and are very much active with your strategy and operations.

A good strategy to secure a lead investor that will establish the
terms of your round could be to get this important person on board
first as an advisor. This will be a great opportunity to start working
together and to have them more involved. Eventually it will come
out of this person investing and leading your round.

Building Momentum

Confidence is everything in business. An investor will not feel confident in your business if your presentation is hesitant or unsure. You must do your best to build momentum and to present as positive an impression of your startup as possible. This isn't about misleading anyone, but it is about sales and attracting a buyer (of sorts).

Creating momentum is a great way to not only build confidence, but to achieve more over a shorter span of time. Momentum comes from leadership, and unless you have a manager who is overseeing your company, that leadership must come from you. Decisions must be implemented with conviction, although these should be carried out via a balanced approach. Some decisions are worth spending a little time on to ensure no costly mistakes are made.

Momentum is also about showing that you have achieved something. If your startup has stagnated and remained in one position for a long period of time, then an investor will want to know why this is the case. On the other hand, if you are continually improving your startup, both conceptually and organizationally, then an investor will know that you are the type of startup founder who doesn't rest on his laurels and is always looking to improve.

When you are in fundraising mode, you want to have as many people as possible talking about your startup, and you also want to be featured as much as possible by the press. This is part of creating the feeling that the train is leaving the station, and it's time for the investor to get on board.

Team Alignment

Another key way to attract an investor is through developing team alignment, also known as synergy. This simply means that your entire organization is pulling in the same direction. It is well organized, and from your management team right down through your company, there is agreement on the direction your startup is taking, with a determined commitment to achieve goals that are widely accepted.

It can be the case that startups with more than one founder may lack direction. Founders can have different ideas about where a business is going and how best to get there. This is a real turnoff for investors. Disagreements slow progress, and while in some cases they are unavoidable, they can be disastrous, resulting in a business that slowly pulls itself apart at the seams.

Dialogue is essential, and debate can be healthy, producing new innovations, but time is always of the essence, and once a decision has been made it should be carried through, even by those who disagree with it.

Remember that over 60 percent of companies go out of business because of founder issues. If you give the impression that there is no alignment, that will raise red flags for investors. Another thing that you want to watch out for is talking over your cofounder during investor meetings. You and your cofounder should never cut each other off.

A united front is essential, especially when attracting investors. Of course there may still be differences of opinion, but progress must be prioritized and that can be achieved only when your startup has the relevant funds to get moving. More than this, much like momentum, team alignment will markedly decrease based on the time it takes to achieve a goal. It can also cut down on costs, as efficiency and economy go hand in hand. If a startup is efficient, low cost, and has a group of experts working together as a cohesive team, it will be an extremely compelling prospect for any number of investors.

Show Your Competitive Advantage

We'll discuss your sales pitch in later chapters, but this aspect cannot be overstressed: You need to be able to show why your business is special. More often than not, there will be other startups that are similar to your own, and so investors can pick the strongest.

You can and should assume that investors have also been in conversations with some of your competitors. They are looking to make a bet on the company that they perceive as having the strongest position in the space.

You have to be able to show why your startup is better than the rest, clearly outlining your competitive advantage in no uncertain terms. This will create confidence in an investor, letting them know that you are good on specifics and that you haven't entered into a marketplace blindly.

If your business has more than one advantage, all the better. You just have to be able to show them. You might have a conceptual advantage because your service/product is innovative and unique. You could have a technological advantage with patent-protected products that your competition simply does not have access to. It could be that you are able to produce a similar service or product to another business but at a much lower cost. Whatever the advantage is, never go into a meeting with a potential investor without having the advantage or advantages in mind, and being ready to pitch them confidently at a moment's notice.

There is nothing that turns off investors more than entrepreneurs who say they do not have any competitors. To paraphrase Mark Cuban, at least 100 other people have thought about your idea. The difference is in the execution.

Know Your Terms

If you do not know how much of your business you are willing to trade for a specific amount of capital, then investors will (usually) not want to be involved.

If you don't know the value of your business, potential investors will infer that you have not undertaken the research to prepare your company for the marketplace. You have to know the valuation of your business, whether it has been assessed by an expert or by yourself. Without solid figures, investors will assume that you are not good with finances, and when your number-one priority is to protect their investment, that's a real issue.

Not knowing your terms can also affect *you*. It's possible that you could give away too much of your startup for too little. You need to know what you're willing to sacrifice to make your startup a success. You might have a figure in your head, but that could change under the influence of nervous tension during negotiations.

That being said, having a solid figure at the outset will give you a foundation from which to build a strong negotiating stance.

If you do not have a lead investor yet, you should not mention the valuation of your business. Talk instead about the valuation of other competitors and let that potential lead initiate the negotiation. The last thing you want is to negotiate the terms against yourself.

Vision

I've saved the topic of "vision" until the end of this chapter because it is so crucial to your success.

The vision you have for your startup should be at the center of everything you do. What do you want the company to achieve? What niche do you want it to fill? What is the end goal for you and for your investors? With these questions answered you will have a mental map that can effectively guide the decision-making process.

Vision isn't only about providing a structure or framework on which to build, it is something that can attract investors, and lots of them. It is the single most important facet of your business, one that will create investor confidence. It will increase your ability to convey to a potential investor why they should be involved in your startup.

With a clear vision you can quickly and concisely outline what their capital will be used for. Showing an investor where your business will be in a defined amount of time is central to concluding an investment round, and you will find both in your vision.

As a startup founder it is your job to take the lead, at least at the conception of your business. With a vision in place you can chart a clear course that will impress potential investors; but there are some caveats that need to be addressed.

Vision is not about being able to talk well or present your case with charm. Your vision must be realistic and achievable. An experienced investor will have heard all the promises, but if these estimates are not based in actual facts such as market growth and consumer need, then you will find it more difficult to attract investment.

Projections are all smoke. Who knows where a startup will be in five years? A good example is Slack: They went from being a gaming company without much traction to a multibillion-dollar business within 18 months. You need to be highly articulate. Investors put their money on the long-term potential of the company and the returns they might obtain, and for that reason nailing it on the vision is critical.

Use your vision to prove your case, and if something doesn't hold up to scrutiny, use that information to craft a better, more effective concept of where your startup stands and where you want it to be in the future.

Attracting Investors Requires Patience

It's important to realize when reaching the stage of attracting investors that you need to have already made the preparations required to make your startup something worth investing in. It can take time to get this right, and your pitch or presentation will change as you start to receive feedback and you cover up some of the holes.

Realize that this entire process is organic and must be tailored as you proceed. If you get far with one investor, only to find some aspect of your preparation didn't stand up to scrutiny, go back and fix the issue as best you can so that the next investor sees a stronger proposition.

Most investors will ask you the same questions. I would encourage you to maintain a list of frequently asked questions and have your responses in a form you can quickly access. This way you will be prepared for future meetings and calls.

By constantly evolving your approach and taking the time to prepare correctly, you've worked to ensure that your business will be more secure and successful in the future.

4

Crafting the Pitch

BY NOW YOU SHOULD HAVE a little more clarity on your vision, expectations, and a launch pad for success in fundraising. At this point, what assets do you need to start approaching investors to get that capital? How should they be optimized to propel success?

The Business Plan Problem

Don't even think of launching a startup or asking for funding without a comprehensive business plan that includes the details of your marketing, fundraising, and how you plan to repay financing. But as you're writing up your business plan, be careful—even the best business plans can be virtually useless when it comes to raising capital.

Far too many startups fall into the business plan trap. They spend extensive periods of time, and often resources, to create the perfect business plan. They believe it has to be impeccably polished—and cost a lot of money—to earn them fundraising requests. Often, spending too much time creating a "perfect" business plan costs entrepreneurs and their ventures the first mover advantage, and lots of precious time that could have been spent making sales.

People may request your business plan. Often this is an anti-quated formality. Sometimes it will be used as a tool to judge your experience, effort, organization, and market research, whether you have your cash flow projections right, and whether you are being realistic or just overselling a pipe dream. It's rarely a conversion tool that secures funding. In fact, the decision to give you money is normally made *before* ever looking at the business plan.

The business plan may play a part in up to 10 percent of the funding process (unless it is really terrible).

The rest of the items in this chapter actually make up 90 to 99 percent of the decision to finance a startup.

Why? Let's be honest—most business plans are dull. No one has time to read a business plan unless they have already made the mental decision to fund you, and are just checking the boxes for due diligence. Experienced business pros and investors know that business plans change. In fact, the funding you receive will probably change your plan (often on the spot).

Do invest in a business plan—a good one. But don't confuse it with a marketing tool or pitching tool that will actually help you raise money. Even more than a business plan, I would encourage you to put together an 18-month plan where you show the investor the execution strategy you will follow with the capital that you plan to raise.

Get the Message Straight and Your Team behind It

If you want to glide toward money that will elevate your startup, you have to make sure your message is clear as a bell, and you need to ensure that you have a unified team capable of communicating it.

Messaging is incredibly important. Your copy, your spoken words, your slogans, your taglines, your backstory, and your branding—they all matter. They not only matter in terms of general marketing to attract customers, but also in getting funded, and even in who funds you and on what terms.

Have a crystal-clear picture of exactly who it is you want to connect with, what you want to portray to them, what will resonate with them, and the optimal messaging that will secure the money and terms you seek. Know your target investor better than your competing startups, and at least as well as your customers, and cater to them. Don't just say what they want to hear. Make sure you are also serving investors well. If it is really a good match, and you can deliver, you will be helping them. Intelligently help them to connect the dots to realize that investing in your startup is what they want to do, and that you are a better choice than your competitors. The process of getting the message right requires the following four steps:

1. Define to whom you are speaking
2. Determine how you can win the opportunity to serve them by highlighting that you have exactly what they are looking for
3. Emphasize specific words that will resonate and improve your positioning (and that connection)
4. Get the whole team on the same page

It won't work if only one of the founders has the pitch down, or if cofounders are spreading mixed messages. The same applies to the rest of the team. So get together on this: Get the whole team's input. Pull the best ideas together. Unite them in your internal documents, and ensure everyone is using the same messaging with every person they speak with about the venture. This applies to social media, personal networking—*everything*. Make consistency paramount.

Consistent messaging pulls investors in. You need to have that internal alignment with your team. When big investors come knocking, the due diligence process will include the investor meeting with other members of your team, and you need to be prepared.

For example, you may be a real estate technology company. Odds are that you will want to focus on identifying mostly as either a real estate company that happens to have a great tech edge, or a tech company that has an edge in the real estate world. You need to choose and stick with one, otherwise you might turn off the wrong people.

Think about Google. Google is *not* a search engine. This has been made even clearer with the move to become Alphabet. If Google (or Alphabet) were just a search engine, it would be a monopoly, ripped apart by regulators in days. That would waste trillions of dollars and years of work. As Alphabet Google, the Google search engine is just a tiny project that the company happens to engage in. It's a very useful part, but just one of the many things that drive value and revenues for Alphabet.

What this really comes down to is that investors are buying into your idea, and they are buying into *you*, for the most part. It is often a lot easier to sell the idea, and what could be, than a bunch of paper that puts people to sleep (if they ever find time to get around to reading it).

The Elevator Pitch

While the name is certainly ready for an upgrade, the "elevator pitch" is still considered one of the most important tools for getting funded. It can also help you gain sales and raise awareness of your startup.

So what makes a great elevator pitch and how do you hone yours to optimal conversion capacity?

The Effective Elevator Pitch

- An elevator pitch is simply a quick introduction to your business
- It's around 30 seconds long
- It sparks interest and response
- It's clear
- It's authoritative
- It is about them (your customers), not you
- It highlights your value and what problem you are solving
- It introduces your uniqueness
- It's relatable

Six Quick Tips for Mastering the Elevator Pitch

1. Role-play your pitch with team members, friends, and family
2. Record yourself and tweak it
3. Go listen to other pitches and note what works or doesn't work
4. Check out elevator pitch competitions (some offer up to $10,000 prizes)
5. Document it in your mobile phone, so you won't be at a loss for words
6. Practice, practice, practice until it becomes natural

Do not underestimate the elevator pitch. Make sure the whole team is armed with it. This is your key to unlock the gates to capital. It can be used in person in actual elevators, online, over the phone, by text message, and in email. Multiple startup founders claim that emailing a simple elevator pitch to Mark Cuban resulted in hundreds of thousands, then millions, of dollars for them, as well as free advice from the billionaire investor.

Here's an example pitch: *"I run a crowdfunding portal that gives investors early access to the hottest, prescreened tech startups, and the ability to invest in them in 10 minutes or less from any Wi-Fi connected device, anywhere in the world."*

The Pitch Deck

The vast majority of startups aren't going to get far without a pitch deck. You can ride without an exhaustive business plan, maybe even with a mediocre and roughly delivered elevator pitch. But you aren't going to be taken seriously, or get funding (even if they really want to give it to you) without the pitch deck.

You are going to need two different versions of your pitch deck. One is the version you will send out with all pertinent information, including everything you need to have people understand your story and where you are heading. The second version of the pitch deck will be used during presentations and contain illustrative graphics that will add to your presentation.

If you score with your elevator pitch, then you'll want to have the capability to deliver your pitch deck instantly. Don't make an eager investor wait while you scramble to put one together.

What types of pitch deck do you need for those moments? And what should be in it?

Three minutes, 44 seconds is the average time a venture capitalist spends looking at a pitch deck, according to TechCrunch.[1] A DocuSend and Harvard Business professor study shows that the average deck is 19 pages long.

For a presentation in venues beyond elevators, Guy Kawasaki recommends no more than 10 slides, not using anything smaller than a 30-point font, and keeping presentation time to 20 minutes.[2] I've also heard of companies simply sending a couple of slides to firms like Union Square Ventures and getting funded. In terms of pages and categories, Sequoia Capital recommends including these 10 aspects:

1. Company purpose
2. Problem
3. Solution
4. Why now
5. Market size
6. Product
7. Team
8. Business model
9. Competition
10. Financials

(Note that these are all items that you can easily adapt or extract from your business plan.)

---

[1] http://techcrunch.com/2015/06/08/lessons-from-a-study-of-perfect-pitch-decks-vcs-spend-an-average-of-3-minutes-44-seconds-on-them/#.wcqqmt:o7ZQ.

[2] http://guykawasaki.com/the-only-10-slides-you-need-in-your-pitch.

Food for thought: Many startups don't include terms or the ask in decks. Consider how you can streamline fundraising, or at least position your ask and your negotiating position by standing out in this area. (Just get that obstacle out of the way.) Also look for other areas where competing startups may be weak, or where they are boring to investors. Excel on these slides!

On the ask slide, you also want to be strategic. Do not put a specific amount that you are raising. For example, if you would like to raise $5 million, I would suggest putting a range between $3 million and $5 million. Firms have limitations on their investment thesis when it comes down to the amounts being raised. This means that if you place $5 million in your pitch deck and that firm has a mandate to not invest over $3 million, you will most likely have them pass. By including the range from $3 million to $5 million on the raise amount you are also including such firms. For that reason, you want to be attractive to as many targets as possible, so go with ranges instead of specific amounts.

The three keys to powerful pitch decks that get funded:

1. Clear and simple
2. Compelling
3. Easy to act on

A Harvard Business study proclaims there is no correlation between getting funded and the volume of decks sent out. Rather, it is a matter of getting your pitch deck into the right investors' hands. This also allows for some tweaking and customization.

So what should your deck look like?

Awesome, Effective Pitch Deck Design

First, and this can't be repeated enough: Invest in a great pitch deck!

Love it or hate it, the great and terrible news is that your startup and fundraising efforts can all depend on the success of your pitch deck. You can have the best, most-needed product or service ever conceived, and be the most qualified and earnest team out there. But if your deck doesn't shine, you are going to have a difficult time raising funds and gaining any traction. At best, you'll have to work a lot harder and longer at it than everyone else. And that's tiring and expensive. A couple of teenagers with no experience but an exciting idea and a great-looking deck can land millions in a matter of weeks, even with a weak business plan. That might seem unfair, but that is how it is, period.

If you want to be competitive in this arena, look at what's trending in pitch deck styles today. Websites like Pitchenvy.com have good examples. Don't be afraid to be different, but don't make yourself look outdated, either. Treat it like a resume. Hopefully you'll never need to seek a job again, but if you did, you wouldn't dust off a 10-year-old resume and spread it around without checking up on current trends, what employers are looking for, and what the best candidates are doing. So run a little reconnaissance. Check out pitch deck templates online, go to pitch nights, and look up some of the publicly posted decks of those that have raised millions with theirs. The fast way to do this is to go to bestpitchdecks.com where you'll discover everything from Airbnb's $2 million pitch deck, to Facebook's original deck, and LinkedIn's B series pitch deck.

It's also worth checking out Headout's amazing visual pitch deck. Via Business Insider Joshua Reeves is an angel who offers a template of his ZenPayroll pitch deck (which landed him $6.1 million in two weeks).[3]

If you are going after serious money like this, it's not a bad idea to ask someone with a high-level understanding of sales psychology to take a look at your deck. A couple of tweaks to images, placement, and words could make a multimillion-dollar difference.

When it comes to design, amazing visuals are great for building emotion—just don't sacrifice clarity. And perhaps most important—but so often overlooked—is that once you've delivered a compelling pitch presentation, ensure that it is easy for investors to take action.

---

[3] www.businessinsider.com/seed-round-pitch-deck-tempate-2013-8?op=1

If you have a crowdfunding campaign, running a direct link should take investors right to a button where they can invest on the spot. If giving a live presentation, you might even go as far as layering the slides with augmented reality so they can scan the screen and get right to that page from their mobile devices.

At a bare minimum, there shouldn't just be basic contact information but also social handles and URLs so that they can instantly follow you, and share you and your presentation with other investors. Don't rely on the hope of connecting for a follow-up conversation. If you can, get real action in the moment. As you're sending your pitch deck around, you never know how many times it may be forwarded.

The One Pager

The one pager brings the whole pitch and all of the elements in this chapter together on one piece of paper or one screenshot. Even when business plans are requested and used (as in commercial finance and in applying for a business loan), entrepreneurs will first be asked to provide a brief executive summary. A one-page executive summary pulls together all of the components.

Airbnb's one pager is an excellent example. The one 8.5 × 11-inch page that the Airbnb CEO revealed to Fast Company has the $20 billion company's entire game plan to take over the world of hospitality in multiple industry tangents on just one page.[4]

A one-page summary of your pitch deck simplifies your fundraising request, making it easy to understand and easy to share and review. Think about crowdfunding. Millions are now raised on crowdfunding portals based on one page on the web.

The one pager is effectively a distilled business plan, pitch deck, mission statement, and tool for uniting the team, and takes thought, skill, and practice. Get your data, messaging, elevator pitch, and visuals together, and boil it down to one winning, multimillion-dollar page.

---

[4] www.fastcompany.com/3027107/punk-meet-rock-airbnb-brian-chesky-chip-conley.

5

The Due Diligence Package

ONCE YOUR PITCH COLLATERAL STARTS working, you need to be prepared to back it up and immediately move forward.

Bloomberg Business reports that two thirds of the deals made on the TV show *Shark Tank* end up falling apart.[1] The funding never happens. This can often be because the due diligence blows holes in the pitch, or other red flags pop up. Sometimes entrepreneurs say that investors simply never show up and follow through. In one case, an entrepreneur who was offered $1 million wasn't prepared to sign at that exact moment, and within 30 days the deal unraveled.

The time to polish your due diligence package is now, not after you begin generating interest. Some of the items in your package can be created and commissioned only by your organization. Others can be hunted down by prospective investors. But do you really want to be the startup that is difficult to finance? Do you want to leave it up to chance or Google to determine what they see, and if it is you or the next startup in line to actually get funded? No? Then make sure you have a strong due diligence package ready to roll out.

---

[1] www.bloomberg.com/bw/articles/2014-07-15/shark-tank-do-two-thirds-of-deals-fall-apart.

Some experienced investors will have a comprehensive checklist of items they need, or things they need to review. Others, especially inexperienced new angels, may request these items piece by piece. That can drag out the process, and potentially sabotage the entire round. It is far better to have a comprehensive package to provide, and this will say a lot about your thoroughness, efficiency, and understanding of what is important to the investor. It's a chance to really get ahead of other competing startups and secure the capital faster.

The due diligence process is really all about clarity in these four areas:

1. People
2. The product
3. Market
4. The deal

So what should be in a startup due-diligence package?

Here are some of the items that may be requested when it comes to due diligence. Note that some investors will have very brief checklists. Others can have checklists that are seven or more pages long.

Sample Startup Due Diligence Checklist

✓ Key team member bios and resumes
✓ Market size
✓ SWOT analysis
✓ Patents
✓ Technology used
✓ Financial statements (three years)
✓ Information on who is providing accounting services
✓ Valuation
✓ Capitalization table
✓ Exit strategy

✓ Company articles of incorporation and certificate of good standing
✓ Organization charts
✓ List of places the company does business in
✓ Credit reports
✓ Background checks
✓ Inventory and assets list
✓ Financial forecasts
✓ Cash flow projections
✓ Details of current funding, financing, leases, credit, and investors
✓ Bank statements
✓ Trademarks and copyrights
✓ Employee and contractor agreements
✓ Insurance documents
✓ License and permit documentation
✓ Tax returns and receipts
✓ Marketing plan
✓ Brand style guide
✓ List of professional and legal consultants used
✓ Offering documents

If you really want to be prepared, I would recommend that you create comprehensive folders on Google Drive or Dropbox that you can share easily with investors. To make sure you have everything for the due diligence process in order to speed things up for investors, you will need all the items listed below. If you have all the documents listed within the folders, then you should be good to go. Make sure you consult with your legal counsel, as well.

1. Organization:
   ☐ 1.01 Certificate of Incorporation (or equivalent) and all amendments and restatements
   ☐ 1.02 Bylaws (or equivalent), as currently in effect

- ☐ 1.03 List of all business names used by or registered for use by the Company
- ☐ 1.04 List of any and all subsidiaries and affiliates of the Company and jurisdiction of formation
- ☐ 1.05 List of all jurisdictions in which the Company owns or leases (either as lessor or lessee) assets or has done so since incorporation
- ☐ 1.06 List of all jurisdictions in which the Company is qualified as a foreign entity, has applied for such qualification, or has substantial contacts
- ☐ 1.07 Minutes, including minutes of meetings of the board of directors, board committees, or the shareholders (or any equivalents); written consents of any of the foregoing in lieu of a meeting; and all materials distributed to the board, board committees, and the shareholders (or any equivalents) at any meeting
- ☐ 1.08 List of any business acquisitions or dispositions made by the Company
- ☐ 1.09 List of all persons who have been or who currently are officers or directors (or equivalent)
2. Capitalization and Securityholders:
   - ☐ 2.01 List of Company securities authorized and outstanding that indicates the holders, amounts and classes or series of such securities, and copies of securities transfer books and stock ledgers
   - ☐ 2.02 Agreements to issue and/or register securities
   - ☐ 2.03 Agreements relating to voting of securities, preemptive rights, restrictions on transfers, rights of first refusal, and any other grants of rights in respect of the Company's securities
   - ☐ 2.04 All warrants, options, or other agreements relating to rights to acquire securities of the Company or requiring the issuance and/or registration of such securities
   - ☐ 2.05 All plans and grant or award documents for any stock option, stock bonus, stock purchase, or other

equity-based compensatory programs for employees, consultants, advisors, and/or directors (or equivalent)

☐ 2.06 Any agreements with "finders" or which purport to obligate the Company to compensate any person or entity in connection with a financing transaction

☐ 2.07 Private placement memoranda, investment letters, questionnaires, and other documents relating to any offering of securities of the Company

☐ 2.08 Copies, front and back, of all stock certificates and stock powers

☐ 2.09 List of any copies of closing binders of each and every prior equity financing (including debt convertible into equity)

3. Financial Statements and Audits:

☐ 3.01 Financial statements for the past three years

☐ 3.02 Schedule of liabilities (contingent or otherwise) not reflected in the most recent financial statements

☐ 3.03 List of any change in accountants and/or auditors since incorporation

☐ 3.04 Copies of audit letters from counsel to auditors since incorporation

4. Taxes:

☐ 4.01 List of all domestic and foreign jurisdictions in which the Company remits sales, use, income, franchise, property, or other taxes

☐ 4.02 Tax returns (federal, state, and local) of the Company since incorporation

☐ 4.03 Reports filed and material correspondence with any and all tax authorities, including the IRS since incorporation

5. Employees, Salaries, and Labor Disputes:

☐ 5.01 All collective bargaining agreements, employment agreements, offer letters, consulting agreements, severance agreements, noncompete or nonsolicit agreements, change-in-control agreements, and intellectual property

transfer agreements, nondisclosure, or confidentiality
agreements to which the Company is a party and list
of any of the foregoing agreements currently contemplated or about to be entered into by the Company

☐ 5.02 Summary of labor disputes, requests for arbitration,
organizational proceedings, grievance proceedings, and
similar matters and history of recent union negotiations

☐ 5.03 List of all employees indicating each employee's
division, title, function, industry experience and earnings, and whether each such person is an officer and/or
director (or equivalent) of the Company

☐ 5.04 List of all employees terminated since incorporation and the reason for such termination, and indicate
whether each such employee has signed a release (and
provide a copy of signed release)

☐ 5.05 Termination procedures, policies, and a sample
termination letter

6. Employment Policies and Employee Benefits:

☐ 6.01 All personnel manuals, employee handbooks, and
documents relating to employment policies and
procedures

☐ 6.02 Any affirmative action plan(s)

☐ 6.03 Policies and practices regarding compensation for
all employees not earning a straight salary (i.e., bonuses,
commissions, overtime, premium pay, shift differentials,
etc.)

☐ 6.04 Policies for fringe benefits, perquisites, holidays,
vacation, and severance pay

☐ 6.05 Incentive, bonus, deferred compensation, profit-
sharing, and nonqualified pension plans

☐ 6.06 Employee health and welfare plans, whether
insured or self-insured, including most recent Summary
Plan Description for each

☐ 6.07 All Form 5500 Series Annual Financial Reports
and summary annual reports (including all supporting

schedules and audit reports) for each employee-benefit plan described in 6.06 above and 6.08 below

☐ 6.08 Each tax-qualified retirement plan and any related trusts or insurance contracts (as amended to date) and most recent Summary Plan Description for each

☐ 6.09 Most recent IRS Determination Letter for each tax-qualified benefit plan

7. Financial Commitments:

☐ 7.01 All indentures, loan, and note agreements (whether demand, term, installment, or other) and line of credit arrangements, whether bank loans, industrial revenue bonds, mortgages, or other and whether secured or unsecured, and all documents evidencing other material financing arrangements, including sale and leaseback arrangements, installment purchases, letters of credit, capital, and leveraged leases and receivables securitizations

☐ 7.02 Summaries of compliance with the instruments described in 7.01 above (including indication of whether defaults are presently anticipated for future periods) and all communications with lenders

☐ 7.03 Guarantees for the benefit of or by the Company

☐ 7.04 List of loans to or from security holders, employees, officers, directors (or equivalent), or any of their immediate family members

☐ 7.05 Contractual obligations relating to termination of employment

☐ 7.06 List of all outstanding indebtedness of the Company detailing amount and effective interest rates of such indebtedness

☐ 7.07 Schedule of all liens and encumbrances to which the property and assets of the Company are subject

8. Consents:

☐ 8.01 List of all material consents required to be obtained by or on behalf of the Company to complete the proposed transaction, specifying the name of the entity or individual from whom consent is required and the agreements under which required and the reason why such consent is required

9. Permits and Licenses; Compliance:

☐ 9.01 All material permits and licenses (including, without limitation, environmental permits and licenses) needed by the Company

☐ 9.02 Description of any regulatory and compliance issues the Company has faced, currently faces, or anticipates facing (including, without limitation, FDA, HIPAA)

☐ 9.03 Information related to potential regulatory or product liability claims or actions that the Company may face

☐ 9.04 If applicable, written policies and guidelines regarding protection of personal health information and related privacy policies

10. Insurance:

☐ 10.01 All insurance contracts, including director-and-officer liability (or equivalent), automobile, general liability, environmental liability, key person (whether or not owned by the Company), and products liability; list of and summaries of insurance claims, disputes with insurance companies or denials of insurance coverage that are currently pending or have occurred since incorporation; and list of insurance claims paid against occurrence policies

☐ 10.02 Workers' compensation documentation

☐ 10.03 Vendor liability endorsements

☐ 10.04 List of any time the Company has ever been declined for a policy or of any time an insurance company has declined to provide a key person policy requested by or on behalf of the Company (whether the policy was to be owned by the Company or not)

11. Litigation:

☐ 11.01 List of and status of pending and threatened claims, litigation, administrative, or other proceedings and governmental investigations involving the Company or, to the extent that they relate to performance of corporate duties (whether for the Company or any third party), any of the directors (or equivalent) or officers or relating to any product manufactured or distributed by the Company and list of counsel presently and previously handling such matters

☐ 11.02 List of outstanding judgments or decrees against the Company and, to the extent that they relate to performance of corporate duties, any of the directors (or equivalent) or officers

☐ 11.03 List of all consent decrees, settlement agreements, injunctions, and similar matters involving the Company and, to the extent that they relate to performance of corporate duties (whether for the Company or any third party), any of the directors (or equivalent) or officers

☐ 11.04 List of all pending and threatened claims, litigation, administrative or other proceedings, and governmental investigations involving any Key Person (defined to mean any founder, officer, or director or key employee of the Company) during the past five years

☐ 11.05 List of any and all bankruptcies and license revocations or suspensions or censures or prohibitions on involvement in the sale or trading of securities or commodities in which any Key Person has been involved, if in effect during the past five years

12. Intellectual Property:

☐ 12.01 Patents, trademarks, service marks, copyrights, trade names, trade secrets, and other intangible assets owned or used by the Company (including domestic or foreign applications, registrations, licenses, and assignments)

☐ 12.02 Opinions relating to patents (including right to use, patentability, blocking patents, infringement, and validity) and opinions relating to trademarks (including registrability, infringement, and validity) and opinions relating to other intellectual property

☐ 12.03 List of all software programs owned by the Company that are (a) used internally by the Company in its business operations or (b) made available by the Company for use by customers

☐ 12.04 List of all software programs owned by third parties that are (a) used internally by the Company in its business operations (other than noncustom, mass-marketed software products licensed under a "shrink wrap" agreement) or (b) made available by the Company for use by customers, indicating in each case the owner of and nature of the Company's right to use such intellectual property

☐ 12.05 License agreements relating to intellectual property under which the Company is licensor or licensee (including "shrink wrap" software products to the extent related to the products developed by the Company) and list of any obligations to pay or rights to receive royalties

☐ 12.06 Documentation alleging infringement of third-party intellectual property by the Company or relating to alleged or actual third-party infringement of the Company's intellectual property

☐ 12.07 Secrecy, confidentiality, nondisclosure, and assignment of inventions agreements with employees, consultants, or independent contractors and list of any employees, consultants, or independent contractors not covered by such agreements

☐ 12.08 Written policies and guidelines distributed to employees regarding protection of proprietary items, technical data, marketing data, or confidential information used by the Company in its business operations

☐ 12.09 Documentation relating to third-party development and testing of the Company's products, services, and proprietary products and information

- [ ] 12.10 List of any open source or community source code incorporated into any of the Company's software products or products under development
- [ ] 12.11 List of all liens and encumbrances upon the Company's intellectual property

13. Property, Plant, and Equipment:
    - [ ] 13.01 List of all real property currently and formerly owned by the Company
    - [ ] 13.02 List of all real property currently and formerly leased to or by the Company
    - [ ] 13.03 All leases and subleases regarding real property and material amounts of personal property leased to or by the Company
    - [ ] 13.04 All material agreements encumbering real or personal property of the Company, including, without limitation, mortgages, deeds of trust, and security agreements
    - [ ] 13.05 All material equipment leases involving the Company, including capitalized or financing leases

14. Environmental Matters:
    - [ ] 14.01 All notices of violation or enforcement activity relating to any domestic or foreign environmental laws received since incorporation or otherwise unresolved at present
    - [ ] 14.02 All "potentially responsible party" notices, Section 104(e) (i.e., 42 U.S.C. §9604(e)) requests or other documents relating to possible liability under CERCLA, onsite or offsite

15. Other Contracts:
    - [ ] 15.01 All contracts, agreements, or arrangements restricting the nature or geographic scope of the Company's business
    - [ ] 15.02 All contracts, agreements, or arrangements between the Company and any officer, director (or equivalent), security holder, or any of their immediate family members

- ☐ 15.03 All contracts, agreements, or arrangements between the Company and management or key personnel
- ☐ 15.04 All secrecy, confidentiality, and nondisclosure agreements between the Company and employees or third parties and list of any employees not covered by such agreements
- ☐ 15.05 All indemnification contracts, agreements, or arrangements for officers and directors (or equivalent)
- ☐ 15.06 All contracts, agreements, or arrangements between the Company and any of its subsidiaries or affiliates
- ☐ 15.07 All commission, brokerage, and agency contracts, agreements, or arrangements to which the Company is a party
- ☐ 15.08 All joint venture, partnership, corporate alliance, collaboration, and similar contracts, agreements, or arrangements to which the Company is a party
- ☐ 15.09 All executed closing documents relating to any merger, acquisition, or disposition by the Company (whether consummated or not)
- ☐ 15.10 All marketing contracts, agreements, or arrangements, including sales agent, representative, dealer, distributor, consignment, consultant, pricing, and advertising agreements, to which the Company is a party
- ☐ 15.11 All material supply, requirements, purchase, or sales contracts, agreements, or arrangements to which the Company is a party
- ☐ 15.12 All material licensing and royalty contracts, agreements, or arrangements to which the Company is a party
- ☐ 15.13 All government contracts, agreements, or arrangements to which the Company is a party
- ☐ 15.14 All contracts, agreements, or arrangements relating to the Company's securities to which the Company is a party, including, without limitation, subordination agreements, standstill agreements, stock option plans,

forms of stock option agreements, and agreements pursuant to which the Company has agreed to issue or to register securities

☐ 15.15 All contracts relating to the operation of the Company's website

☐ 15.16 All other contracts, agreements, or arrangements that provide for the aggregate payment or receipt by the Company of $10,000 or more

☐ 15.17 All other material contracts, agreements, or arrangements

16. Miscellaneous:

☐ 16.01 All other documents and information that are significant with respect to any portion of the Company's business or that should be considered and reviewed by prospective investors in the Company

Cap Tables

Of all the above cap tables or capitalization tables, there are few that founders will have had experience with before. This breaks down who the owners are, who has stock and options, what rounds of funding you anticipate to rate, and how much shares should be worth at each stage.

Thankfully there have been a number of other startups that have launched to provide quick and easy methods to use cap table tools and apps. You may want to check out some of the following.

- Captable.io
- Certent
- Sharewave
- Capshare

The service that I would definitely recommend is EShares. They are a little bit more advanced and there are some costs involved, but they are great. In essence, EShares is a modern equity management company that helps with cap table management, 409A valuations, ASC 718 reporting, and employee liquidity. It will help make your life much easier and reduce legal costs, especially postfinancing.

References and Background Checks

References and background checks are a crucial part of the fundraising and due diligence process. Do not underestimate this. Sadly, too, many founders rush ahead without anticipating this scrutiny. Think about it. Investors are really investing in you. You (and your founding team) are the most important part of the equation. And there are also legal requirements that founders and business owners must follow in order to raise funds, especially when it comes to the protections of SEC exemptions for crowdfunding and selling securities.[2] This means having no "bad actors" on board.

This makes it critical to clean up any dirt, get polished up, and make sure you shine. Just imagine you are running for president. If you've just gotten out of prison on a triple homicide charge, or are still wearing an ankle bracelet while on parole for a securities fraud indictment, this is probably not the ideal moment to be attempting to raise big VC money. That doesn't mean that fundraising is impossible, or that you should put the brakes on your startup business idea by any means. But do be alert to the restrictions. Everyone makes mistakes, and deserves a second chance, but every business should invest in cleaning up anything derogatory.

Potential red flags here may include civil and criminal judgments, cease and desist orders, bankruptcy, foreclosure, bad credit, insolvency, and of course those notorious late-night Facebook or LinkedIn posts.

Many of these marks may show up in public records or more thorough background checks. However, expect investors and third parties to hit the web to do some digging, and actively pursue references. This is a good time to settle any collection accounts or

---

[2] www.crowdcheck.com/content/bad-actor-reports.

legal issues you have, as well as rebuilding any bridges you may have burnt in the past.

The social media aspect shouldn't be news to any serious businessperson. If you haven't yet, ask people to stop tagging you online. Ask them to remove unflattering images and posts. Clean house when it comes to your friends, circles, user handles, networks you are on, online comments you have made, and so forth. This is not the week to have your Ashley Madison account leaked to the public.

Make sure the connections that you have on LinkedIn, Google+, Twitter, and Facebook represent a promising founder, and a good risk. Expect each and every one of them to be contacted and asked for a reference. This is also a good time to request additional recommendations on LinkedIn, and Google reviews.

Then hit Google. What do search results return for your name, your cofounder's names, key workers names, and your startup? Make sure you check from different devices, browsers, and search engines, too, so that you are aware of any discrepancies.

At least the first three pages of results should be positive and credible ones. If not, it is time for some rapid online reputation management. If you can't erase the bad or mediocre, then at least bury it with new good references. A blog, article marketing, press releases, and more social activity may all be helpful.

The Interview and the Visit

During the due diligence process, your startup may be visited in person. You may meet the investors themselves, insurance representatives, or third-party due diligence experts.

Many entrepreneurs don't anticipate this, but it is a logical step in due diligence to expect. Don't panic. Don't go over the top forking over money for new office digs or decor, and cripple your numbers with new overhead or spending. See these meetings as an opportunity to really stand out from the crowd. Use them as an opportunity to showcase your startup culture and DNA, and what will ensure that you'll keep going when others would fail. Use the due diligence process as a great relationship and confidence building tool, on your own turf.

During this process expect questions like:

- How many people are on the team?
- How are they compensated?
- Have you and they ever been a part of a startup before?
- Is this a full-time or part-time pursuit?
- How many shareholders are there? Who are they?
- How are you going to make money?
- Who are your main competitors?
- How much are you trying to raise?
- How much are you paying for your space?
- How much did your space design cost?
- Are your existing investors reinvesting?

In some cases most of the items we've covered in this chapter will be a matter of simply checking a box. In other cases investors may use a ranking system to evaluate you. Some investors will be coming in with the mindset that they want to say yes, and are just confirming that decision.

Others go in with a mindset of finding ways to say no. When it comes to questions like these there may be no right answer. Different investors may have their preferences, but overall this is about testing your competency.

No startup is going to be perfect, and a lot may change after receiving significant funding. So, have answers. Know where the potential holes in your plans and venture are. Have answers about what you are doing to investigate and solve them.

Find Balance

Be vigilant and thorough in preparing for due diligence, but don't let it derail your startup, just as with the entire fundraising process. Via

Entrepreneur Magazine, angel investor and startup advisor Martin Zwilling warns founders not to get carried away and exhaust their teams in the process.[3]

Do your best, but don't let it stall your startup's momentum and mojo. Don't let it drain you or your resources.

---

[3] www.entrepreneur.com/article/241512.

6

Sources of Capital

WHAT FUNDRAISING OPTIONS ARE THERE for startups today?

There are at least 10 different sources of funding for startups, from seed money to working capital. What are they, how are they different, what are the pros and cons, and which is right for you and the current stage of your company?

Bootstrapping

In recent years, the explosion of "bootstrapping" startups became the epicenter of many other trends and industries from house hacking to digital nomads, to the ramen diet (and restaurants), coworking spaces, and numerous blogs and guides. The power of bootstrapping should not be underestimated, but it isn't always as glamorous as tech media often portrays.

Bootstrapping really means launching and growing a startup with resources that you already have, and pulling yourself up with a little grit and sweat equity. Technically you could be bootstrapping if you have a six-figure retirement you can tap. Most are working with substantially less, although it's also true there are plenty of startups that are now worth billions that were started with $1,000 or less.

As a good example, I like the story of dating site Plenty of Fish. The founder bootstrapped the business by paying operating costs with Google ads and barely raised money from outside large institutional investors. The company was recently acquired for $575 million in cash by Match Group—definitely a one-of-a-kind success story.

Bootstrapping at the start has many benefits, even for those hoping to raise billions in capital later on. But underestimating the cons can be perilous for startups and solo entrepreneurs. From my perspective, the number-one benefit is that you do not need to report to investors who have expectations, and you are not diluting your equity position.

A Spartan lifestyle is the norm for many bootstrapping entrepreneurs. Supplementing a ramen diet with cans of cold tuna and warm hand-mixed protein shakes while sleeping in a car in Silicon Valley isn't for everyone. Those with a little more in resources can trim the fat from their personal budgets with public transport, creative living arrangements, and forgoing the $10 frothy lattes unless they are meeting with prospects. Master this and you will certainly learn to maximize every dollar in life and business. You'll also find a new appreciation for everything, including a new level of gratitude for the privilege of being able to launch and run your own business. This is a valuable and prized mentality and spirit when it comes to leaders of all sizes of business.

This spirit and financial wizardry can be appealing to other capital sources and investors. That is, providing you can portray that you will continue this level of frugality and precision when it comes to working with their money. Because the truth is that if your product, service, or business works without money, more capital can add to the profit margins and top line revenues. If it doesn't work without money, it may never be sustainable, no matter how much money is poured into it.

Besides cramping your lifestyle it is also essential for founding entrepreneurs to recognize the very real implications, limitations, and risks blind bootstrapping can have on a startup venture. While too much money in the hands of the inexperienced and undisciplined can be a negative thing, too little capital is, unquestionably, one of the most common reasons why businesses fail.

In order to make bootstrapping work for you, you'll have to master the following.

- Guerrilla marketing
- Budgeting
- Time management
- Hiring
- Growth hacking

Are these your strengths? Are they the strengths of one of your cofounders? If not, long-term bootstrapping may not be for you. It takes time for even the greatest products and business models to scale, build their own capital, and sustain themselves. And if you wait until you go flat broke, that can be a big turn-off to other sources of capital. All you've proven is that your idea wasn't financially viable. Or at least that you don't have the skills to make it profitable.

So understand the good, the bad, and the ugly of bootstrapping. Embrace it. But respect its limitations.

Credit Cards

If the cash you have on hand or capital you can add as you go along simply isn't enough, there are always credit cards. This might be an appealing option to the bootstrapping entrepreneur who wants to go it alone. It may not be the most prudent financial choice, and your financial advisor would certainly be cringing at the idea, but it has been done.

The four keys to successfully using credit cards to finance your startup:

1. Set borrowing limits
2. Preset a timeline to pay off your borrowing
3. Protect your credit score
4. Prioritize repaying balances

There are several dangers of using credit cards to fund a startup, including the following.

- Depleting your credit score and profile
- Getting into the bad habit of maintaining high amounts of debt
- Borrowing at outrageous interest rates
- Being poised for failure if the market changes

All too often founders get into the habit of maintaining high balances. They never pay them back. And high interest rates and payments can eat up much of the profits coming in from a young business.

Where it gets really precarious is when high balances crush credit scores. That prevents further credit line increases or borrowing, and can turn off other potential capital sources. When credit scores dive, or the economy turns south, banks are quick to slash credit limits. That can put an instant freeze on credit and cash flow. That can kill a young business just as it is beginning to take off.

Whether you are already affluent and have a black Amex, or have to start out with secured credit cards from Capital One, there are options. Just make sure that you set boundaries in advance and have an exit plan from the debt.

Business Loans

Small business loans from banks used to be the first place for entrepreneurs to apply. Anyone who has attempted to walk into a local branch of a big bank chain knows that this isn't an easy option anymore. Banks rarely make loans to brand new startups—at least in the form of the traditional small business loan. But there are options.

There are some very good reasons to seek business credit from the start.

- It demonstrates you are serious about making this a business, not a hobby

- Separates your personal and business credit and assets
- Reduces personal liability
- Adds tangible value to the business itself
- Potential tax benefits

Potential options for business capital from traditional bank and lender sources:

- Business credit cards
- Business lines of credit
- SBA loans

Some of these options are available for newer businesses. This is especially true if founders have a track record, tangible collateral like real estate is involved, or they have large deposits in an institution.

Two caveats to keep in mind:

1. Most traditional banks won't lend unless you really don't need the money
2. Beware of shady line of credit offers that can be expensive

Friends and Family

Raising capital for a startup can be very controversial. On one hand it can be one of the very best sources of early-stage startup funding. On the other hand it can be one of the biggest regrets many entrepreneurs will have to live with. So why do it? How do you minimize the cons?

The pros of fundraising from family and friends:

- Easiest and fastest investors to obtain funding from
- Borrowing or fundraising costs are minimal
- More attractive terms
- More slack when you need it
- Less pressure, which can decrease mistakes
- Helping your friends and family

Raising capital from friends and family is about more than just bringing more money in. It's about giving, sharing, and strengthening your venture from the ground up. If your friends and family don't believe in your venture, you are going to have a hard time convincing others to back it, or buy it.

Other investors are certainly going to want to know why your friends and family didn't want to invest with you, too. If you are on to something great, and you are convinced it will be a success, why wouldn't you want your friends and family, those whom you love most, to participate in and benefit from your idea? What if a member of your family or close circle of friends launched the next multi-billion-dollar startup and never offered you a chance to get in? You'd probably be pretty hurt.

Opportunities like these can be life-changing for friends and family. It's not just about making them rich. It's about setting them up to be able to provide for their families.

So why do so many hold back from throwing this lifeline to those they care about most?

No founder launches a startup believing it will fail. Statistics Brain shows that small business failure rates have declined as of 2015. Research compiled from the University of Tennessee, Bradley University, the Small Business Development Center, and *Entrepreneur Weekly* shows that as many as 58 percent of businesses in some industries are still operating after four years. That is in stark contrast to a decade earlier when over 90 percent of small businesses were expected to flop soon after launch.[1] But losing investment capital given by friends and family can be devastating for relationships. And relationships are far more valuable than any amount of funding. They are priceless. No entrepreneur wants to sacrifice them.

Just imagine how awkward Christmas dinners could be. They could become more of a shareholders' meeting than a proper dinner with the people that you love.

---

[1] www.statisticbrain.com/start-up-failure-by-industry/.

On the bright side, asking for assistance from family can help entrepreneurs to really put their all into their ventures. And it can increase the number of individuals invested in making a startup work. If properly approached, any risk of tension can be lowered, too.

New Jersey–based fund manager Fuquan Bilal says that he crosses this bridge by proving his theories work and producing results with his own money first. Only then will he permit friends and family to participate, with amounts small enough so that any disappointment won't cause them to stop talking to him.

In order to stay organized and businesslike and protect everyone involved, document everything clearly and make sure everyone understands and is comfortable with the risks. Make sure you tell them there is a high probability of them not seeing that money ever again and ask them if what they're willing to give is money that they can really afford to lose.

Crowdfunding

While some individuals are just now discovering crowdfunding, it has been online since at least 2008. Since then, crowdfunding has evolved to funding some of the most notable new startups and technological developments, and has been used by some of the world's best-known brands, like Hard Rock.

In reality the principles of crowdfunding have been around for hundreds and possibly thousands of years. It is really about individuals coming together to finance a project or business startup. The roots of crowdfunding go back to Ireland in the 1700s and Jonathan Swift, "the father of microcredit." In the times of the Tudors, kings and queens of different European nations came together to combine their resources for various campaigns. Hundreds of years before that time, the great empires of history brought together various crowds to conquer new territory, build roads, craft merchant fleets, construct colosseums, and more.

Today most notable developments and businesses are the product of some form of crowdfunding. Even Warren Buffett's investment juggernaut Berkshire Hathaway, and the companies it owns and operates, is effectively a form of crowdfunding.

What most people refer to as "crowdfunding" today is online web portals that facilitate and streamline project promotion, and the raising of capital. There are now hundreds of crowdfunding platforms supporting different forms of crowdfunding, and different niches. Some specialize in real estate, others in well-vetted startup investments, and others in raising money for personal items like food and weddings. Two types of crowdfunding are donation crowdfunding and equity crowdfunding.

Donation crowdfunding is epitomized by Kickstarter and Indiegogo. These crowdfunding portals allow promoters to raise money in the form of donations in exchange for unique perks.

Via donation-based crowdfunding, donors or backers do not enjoy any ownership or participation in the ongoing profits of a campaign or business launch. Most individuals donate to facilitate the development of things they care about, to support causes, and for the prestige of being among the first to launch a new product. The most-funded Kickstarter as of the first quarter of 2015 was the Pebble smartwatch. Between two campaigns Pebble raised over $30.5 million. Not bad for giving away products and keeping all your equity.

In the event you are able to raise money without giving equity away, I would absolutely encourage you to go this route. Donation-based crowdfunding is used nowadays to presell products. It works particularly well if you are selling hardware products or something tangible that you can give in exchange for the contributions.

Some of the benefits of donation crowdfunding include the following.

- Access to capital
- A great marketing tool to obtain additional exposure
- Obtaining proof of concept
- It allows to crowdsource the feedback process from potential customers
- Potential free PR

When backers decide to back a campaign, they have arrived at the most important step in the process. This is called the act of impulse, in which the investor takes out his or her wallet and pledges money to your campaign. This act of impulse is the result of the following:

1. Backers connect to the greater purpose of the campaign
2. Backers connect to a physical aspect of the campaign, like the rewards
3. Backers connect to the creative display of the campaign's presentation

However, in the event you are operating a tech-enabled company, it is going to be a little bit complicated to go via this route, as there is only so much that you can offer in exchange for the contributions. Beta test, early access, and T-shirts are definitely not so appealing to this crowd.

Equity crowdfunding is a completely different tool altogether from donation-based crowdfunding. The mechanics of equity crowdfunding platforms appear very similar to donation crowdfunding sites but they are two completely different animals.

Equity crowdfunding enables individual investors, angel groups, and other capital funds to invest in the securities of private companies, and participate in their rising value and profits. Startups and small businesses are able to use these platforms to raise funds from a much broader crowd online, while increasing visibility and credibility, generating buzz, testing the waters, and proving the demand for their product or service.

We dig deeper into equity crowdfunding in our chapter on understanding the JOBS Act. The most successful offerings will be those that find the right platform match for their offering, which connects them with serious, qualified investors. (Data shows that crowdfunding has now become a common precursor to obtaining sizable venture capital and offers from venture capital firms.)

Keep in mind that right now, equity crowdfunding platforms are acting as fillers on offerings. This means that most of the time, the offerings that are shown on the platforms have an offering with terms that have been established by an offline investor. As of today there is a great amount of the offerings that are raised offline, with the online financing being a small portion of the total amounts raised.

Down the line these platforms will start to lead rounds and establish the terms. My feeling is that when such a thing occurs there will be a huge shift in the market and perhaps the picture of early stage financing will change—especially the operational structure of early stage venture capital firms and angel groups.

Angel Investors and Super Angels

High net-worth individuals make up the bulk of the ranks of startup investors. These individuals are often referred to as "angel investors" or "accredited investors." The term *angel investor* comes from investors who financed Broadway shows in the past century.

While an angel is normally an accredited investor, this isn't always true. And not all accredited investors are angels. Together, these individuals both have the finances and desire to provide funding. And for many reasons, they are among the most appealing sources of funding for startup founders.

While there are various levels and definitions of "high net-worth" individuals, accredited investors are defined as those with a net worth of $1 million in assets or more (excluding personal residences), or they have $200,000 in income for the previous two years, or a combined income of $300,000 for married couples. This is all according to the definition established by the Securities and Exchange Commission (SEC).

Angel investors are individuals who invest in startup businesses, normally in the early stages. This tends to be on seed rounds of financing and also Series A rounds. Super angels are those that invest checks north of $500,000 on Series A and up.

Angel investors fill the gap between friends and family, and more formal venture capital funds. Some invest purely for profit. Others look to make an impact with their funds by investing in causes and industries they are really passionate about. This can range from sustainable farming to education and healthcare startups.

Angel investors invest their own money, where the typical amount raised ranges from $150,000 to $2,000,000. Since angel investors are very often individuals who have held executive positions at large corporations, they can often provide fantastic advice and introductions to the entrepreneur, in addition to the funds. A Harvard report provided information on how angel-funded startups had a higher chance of survival.

Angel investments are high risk, which is why this strategy normally doesn't represent over 10 percent of the investment portfolio of any given individual. What angel investors look for is a great team with a good market that could potentially return 10 times their initial investment in a period of five years. The exits, or liquidity events, are for the most part via an initial public offering or an acquisition.

According to the Halo Report, angel investors particularly like startups operating in the following industries: Internet (37.4 percent), healthcare (23.5 percent), mobile and telecom (10.4 percent), energy and utilities (4.3 percent), electronics (4.3 percent), consumer products and services (3.5 percent), and other industries (16.5 percent).

Data collected by the Kauffman Foundation shows that the best estimate for angel investor returns is 2.5 times their investment, even though the odds of a positive return are less than 50 percent, which is absolutely competitive with venture capital returns.

Reaching nearly $23 billion in 2012, angel investors are not only responsible for funding over 67,000 startup ventures annually, but their capital also contributed to job growth by helping to finance 274,800 new jobs in 2012, according to the Angel Market Analysis by the Center for Venture Research at the University of New Hampshire. On the contrary, venture capital firms invest in only 1,000 new companies per year.

While angel investors contribute about five times less capital to startups than VCs, individual investments in startups grew by 36 percent from 2008 to 2012, while venture capital investments dropped by 8 percent, according to Dow Jones VentureSource. The average angel investment grew more than 20 percent from 2011 to 2012, from $70,690 to $85,435, according to the Center for Venture Research.

The dominating geographic area, in terms of number of angel investments, is Silicon Valley; however, Silicon Alley is catching up quickly.

The following list gives six reasons these high net-worth investors are an attractive source of capital for you.

1. They can lend additional value via advice from experience
2. Ability to raise more money through fewer investors and contacts
3. Fewer restrictions on raising money from accredited investors
4. They may put in more money later on
5. "Birds of a feather flock together"—angels can potentially give referrals to other angels
6. Flexibility in terms

Note that a Stanford study[2] reports that 90 percent of all seed and startup capital comes from angel investors.

Angel Groups

Angel investors are increasingly combining to form and join angel groups. According to historical data and the Angel Capital Association, the number of angel groups multiplied from just 10 in 1996 to over 330 in 2013.[3]

---

[2] www.gsb.stanford.edu/ces/resources/angel_financing.html.
[3] www.forbes.com/sites/tanyaprive/2013/03/12/angels-investors-how-the-rich-invest.

Super Angels and angel groups clearly often have much more capacity. And the reduced risk they enjoy as they pool money theoretically aids startups in negotiating terms.

During the past 15 years, angel investors have joined different angel groups in order to get access to quality deals. If you are not a Reid Hoffman, a Ron Conway, or connected somehow to one of the founding members of the startup, it was certainly very hard to gain access and participate unless you were affiliated with one of the angel groups.

Some of the biggest angel groups that are most active include the New York Angels, Houston Angel Network, Alliance of Angels, Golden Seeds, Launchpad Venture Group, Robin Hood Ventures, or Tech Coast Angels, amongst others.

One of the most recent players to join in is my beloved 1000 Angels. 1000 Angels is the world's largest digital-first, invitation-only network for select angel investors. 1000 Angels provides investor education and private investment opportunities to a select group of high net-worth individuals looking for a curated approach to early-stage private-equity investing.

The group of 1000 Angels aims to provide a disciplined approach to angel investing for members, allowing them to build a portfolio of investments. The portfolio approach helps to diversify some of the risks inherent in early-stage investing.

From my biased point of view, 1000 Angels has something that the market did not have before, and that is a great digital experience that lets members and entrepreneurs interact with one another.

Family Offices

Family offices often go unnoticed or unrecognized by many entrepreneurs and startups. But they are a very significant force in the investment world and capital markets, so much so that they effectively lobbied Congress to provide an exemption to family offices under the Dodd-Frank Act. In the *Wall Street Journal* report "How to

Bank Like a Billionaire,"[4] family offices are revealed to cost as much as $1 million a year to run, and until recently have been the exclusive domain of the $100-million-plus, high net-worth crowd.

We're talking about Rockefeller-level money. Now affluent families with $5 million to $10 million to invest may participate as a part of a multifamily office for efficiency and cost savings. This is a lot of capital that is waiting to be invested, and a source that is often neglected by others.

In my experience, family offices always have a good amount of capital to be invested in high-risk investments like startups. These types of entities make decisions and move very quickly.

Venture Capital

Venture capital (aka VC money) is perhaps the most commonly sought-after type of capital by entrepreneurs today. It can also be the most difficult to land, and takes the most amount of work. If you want to have a clear understanding of the dynamics behind venture capital firms you should read the book *Mastering the VC Game*[5], written by Jeff Bussgang.

The rewards of getting funded by a big venture capital fund can go far beyond the cash and ego boost. But it does normally require investing in a good pitch, pitching materials, getting out to make personal connections, and a lot of time in prospecting. For some this is nothing more than a huge and costly distraction. For others it is the ultimate goal. Getting financing from a VC takes time and multiple conversations.

The Small Business Administration (SBA) describes this type of equity capital as being essential for "successful long-term growth for most businesses."[6]

---

[4] http://webreprints.djreprints.com/1005380530169.html.
[5] Jeffrey Bussgang, *Mastering the VC Game: A Venture Capital Insider Reveals How to Get from Start-up to IPO on Your Terms* (Penguin Group (USA) LLC, April 29, 2010).
[6] www.sba.gov/content/venture-capital.

True venture capital differs in that it is provided by organized funds and entities. These entities pool the funds of angel investors, family offices, sovereign funds, high net-worth individuals, and others. They primarily seek early-stage, high-growth potential investments. While the percentage of funding that VC firms offer may actually be far less than that of individual angel investors, these companies generally seek to make investments in at least the $1 million–plus range.

The National Venture Capital Association says that around 600 to 800 of the 2,000,000 businesses launched in the United States each year obtain VC funding. In turn, this is said to be responsible for more than 10 percent of national private sector jobs, and over 20 percent of GDP.[7]

Finding a good match in a VC firm is critical. Pitching the right matches makes all the difference in terms and the amount of resources expended before securing funding.

Paul Graham of Y Combinator notes that there is a massive disparity between VC firms. The largest and best known can be tougher to negotiate with, yet the mere association can help catapult success. Other lesser-known firms may be easier to negotiate with, to acquire better terms. But Graham warns that some firms may tie up founders without providing funding, or can attach negative connotations to a venture. The most successful startups will raise venture capital from multiple VCs.[8]

I would like to caution entrepreneurs here. You do not want to raise venture capital money at an early stage where you are still trying to figure out product and market fit. The reason behind this is mainly due to signaling issues if VCs invest in your seed round but then decide not to invest in your bridge round or Series A round. That would send a very negative message to the market that could ultimately cost you the business.

---

[7] https://en.wikipedia.org/wiki/Venture_capital.

[8] www.paulgraham.com/startupfunding.html.

When you bring onboard VCs that means that you know that if you invest X, you will be able to produce XYZ. If you are not sure, then do not take the money and instead delay until you have a little bit more certainty on the horizon. We will dive deeper into how VCs work later on.

Venture Debt

Venture debt is effectively borrowing to raise working capital and growth capital. This is a valuable source of funding that doesn't mean giving up more ownership or diluting equity.

Venture debt financing differs from other sources of money in that it is normally provided by specialist entities and banks that offer their services to funded startups and growing businesses. They understand the dynamics of a startup, and will often lend, even though asset collateral may be weak.

These lenders offset risk by tying loans to accounts receivable, equipment, or rights to purchase equity in a default. A healthy startup can find venture debt attractive in order to allow more time between equity funding rounds so that more notable milestones can be achieved. These funds can also help speed through milestones to reach the IPO stage faster. However, it is critical for founders to ensure their early funding term sheets allow for venture debt to be used as they grow.

All of the above sources of capital can be used by startups. It is normally not a matter of choosing one or two, but rather putting them in the right order to maximize funding, venture potential, and achieving the best exit or IPO.

7

Understanding the VC Game

VENTURE CAPITAL FIRMS ARE WITHOUT a doubt the muscle behind innovation, as they support the company they may invest in, from the early stages all the way to IPO—especially those with larger funds that have billions of dollars under management.

In this chapter I would like to walk you through the logistics of venture capital firms so that you are able to understand fully how they operate.

Defining Roles in a VC Firm

VC firms have different types of individuals working at the firm. The most junior people want to be analysts. These people are either MBA students in an internship or people that just graduated from school.

The main role of analysts is to go to conferences and to scout deals that might be within the investment strategy of the fund that the VC firm is investing out of. Analysts are not able to make decisions, but they could be a good way to get your foot in the door and to have them introduce you to someone more senior within the firm. However, analysts are for the most part conducting research of the market and studying you and your competitors, so be careful about educating them too much.

The most immediate position after the analyst is the associate. An associate could be either junior or senior. Associates tend to be people with a financial background and with powerful skills in building relationships. Associates do not make decisions in a firm but they can definitely warm up an introduction with individuals involved in the decision making.

Over associates, you will be able to find principals. They are senior people who can make decisions when it comes to investments but they do not have full power in the execution of the overall strategy of the firm. A principal can get you inside the door and be your lead to help bring you through the entire process of receiving funding. Principals are those individuals who are close to making partner. They have power within the firm but cannot be considered the most senior within the firm.

The most senior people within a VC firm are above principals, and are called partners. Partners could be general partners or managing partners. The difference in the title varies depending on whether the individual has only a say in investment decisions or also has a voice in operational decision making. In addition to investments, partners are accountable for raising capital for the funds with which the firm will be investing. Last, venture partners are not involved in the day-to-day operations or investment decisions of the firm. Venture partners have a strategic role with the firm, mainly involving bringing new deal flow that they refer to other partners of the firm. Venture partners tend to be compensated via carried interest, which is a percentage of the returns that funds make once they cash out of investment opportunities.

Another figure in a VC firm is the entrepreneur in residence (EIR). EIRs are mainly individuals that have a good relationship with the VC and perhaps have given the VC an exit, helping them earn cash. EIRs generally work for a year or so with the firm, helping them to analyze deals that come in the door. Ultimately the goal of an EIR is to launch another startup for positive investment.[1]

Investors of VC firms are called limited partners (LPs). LPs are the institutional or individual investors who have invested capital in the funds of the VC firm with which they are investing. LPs include endowments, corporate pension funds, sovereign wealth funds, wealthy families, and funds of funds.

The Process of Getting Funded by a VC

As I've mentioned previously in this book, first and foremost, identify the VC that might be investing within your vertical. There are plenty of tools you can use to identify who might be a fit. (You can use Crunchbase, Mattermark, CB Insights, or Venture Deal.)

Once you have your list of targets, you will need to see who you have in common and close to you who would be in a position to make an introduction. The best introductions come from entrepreneurs who have given good returns to the VC. VCs use these introductions as social proof and the stamp of approval on the relationship. The better the introduction, the better the chance you have of getting funded.

As a next step to receiving the introduction, and in the event there is a genuine show of interest from the VC, you will have a call. Ideally you would want to go straight to the partner to save time, or the goal would be to get an introduction to the partner ASAP. If you are already in communication with the partner after the first call, he or she will ask you to send a presentation if the call goes well and there is interest.

After the partner has reviewed the presentation, she will get back to you (or perhaps her assistant) in order to coordinate a time for you to go to the office and to meet face to face. During this meeting,

---

[1] Jeffrey Bussgang, *Mastering the VC Game: A Venture Capital Insider Reveals How to Get from Start-up to IPO on Your Terms* (Penguin Group (USA) LLC, April 29, 2010).

you'll want to connect on a personal level and to see if you have things in common. The partner will ask questions (which have already been covered in previous chapters). If you are able to address every concern well and the partner is satisfied, then you will be invited to present to the other partners.

The partners meeting is the last step to getting to the term sheet. All the decision-making partners will be in the same room with you. Ideally the partner you have been in communication with has spoken highly of you, unless there have been issues (which you've hopefully resolved by this time).

You'll receive a term sheet if you were able to satisfy the concerns put forward at the partners' meeting. Remember that the term sheet is just a promise to give you financing. It does not mean that you will get the capital. It is a nonbinding agreement. Following the term sheet, the due diligence process begins. It will typically take a VC one to three months to complete the due diligence. Unless there are major red flags, you should be good to go and receive the funds in the bank once all the offering documents have been signed and executed.

How VCs Monetize

VCs make money on management fees and on carried interest. Management fees are generally a percentage of the amount of capital that they have under management. Management fees for the VC are typically around 2 percent.

The other side of making money is the carried interest. To understand this concept, carried interest is basically a percentage of the profits. This is normally anywhere between 20 and 25 percent. It is normally in the largest range if the VC is a top-tier firm such as Accel, Sequoia, or Kleiner Perkins.

In order to cash out and receive the carried interest, the VC needs to have the portfolio of each one of the funds making an exit, which means that the company is acquired or will offer an IPO in which investors are able to sell their position.

Normally exits take between five to seven years, if the company has not run out of money or the founders have not run out of energy. Typically VCs want to sell their positions within eight to 10 years, especially if they are early-stage investors.

Startups are a very risky type of asset class and nine out of 10 will end up failing. For that reason, VCs will go for those companies with the potential of giving them a 10x type of return so that it can help them with the losses of other companies inside their portfolios. If you are not able to project these kinds of returns, a VC might not be the route to follow for financing.

VC Involvement in Your Company

VCs would like to have a clear involvement with your company in order to stay close to their investment and to have a say in major decisions that could impact their returns in the long run.

With this in mind, VCs will normally buy in equity between 15 percent to 45 percent of your company. Normally in earlier stage rounds, it tends to be on the higher end but VCs need to be mindful of the stake they leave with the entrepreneur so that they are still motivated enough to stick around and to continue focusing on the execution.

VCs will request board involvement in return for the investment that they are making in your company. There are two types of board levels. One will be the board of director seat in which they participate in major decisions of the company. This is especially important when it comes to future rounds of financing or merger and acquisition (M&A) transactions.

The other level of board involvement is what is known as board observer, as we discuss in the Term Sheets and Terms chapter.

Understanding the Value a VC Brings

Most VCs say the main reason why an entrepreneur should consider working with a VC is because of the value they can bring to the overall strategy and execution of the business. However, that is far from true.

You will need to do the due diligence in order to really under-stand if a VC is going to add value in addition to capital. This value can be introductions for potential partnerships, their network of other successful founders, or the infrastructure that the firm brings.

The infrastructure could be the most attractive part. VCs like Andreessen Horowitz or First Round Capital have a dedicated team of marketers, recruiters, and other resources to bring to a company they invest in. Ultimately this helps in fueling the growth of the business.

Cutting through the VC Noise

As a founder you want to ask the right questions, which will help you understand if the VC is truly interested in investing, or what style of partners you will be onboarding to your company after the financing round is closed.

If the VC firm has not invested in more than six months in new companies, that indicates that the VC is having trouble closing their next fund or that they are in fundraising mode. If this is the case, move on to the next VC; otherwise the process will be put on hold. Closing a fund typically can take between 12 and 24 months. You always want to choose to work quickly.

Ask how they typically work with portfolio companies. Ask the VC to make an introduction to a few founders from companies that have gone out of business. These questions can provide a complete picture.

In addition, ask about allocations to the options pool for employees of companies your size. (This should be written out in the deal's terms.) If you see they want to allocate over 20 percent on a seed round, or over 10 percent on a Series A round of financing, this could mean they may eventually want to replace the founding team.

Differences between Venture Capital and Private Equity

There is confusion about the differences between venture capital and private equity. Venture capital firms tend to work throughout the life cycles of a company, all the way to the liquidity event, when the startup either gets acquired or goes through an IPO.

VCs are also very much involved in the operational structure. However, the main difference is that VCs invest in people with a greater degree of risk than a traditional private equity (PE) firm. PEs will go more for the numbers. They invest in businesses that are already formed, where the outcome is more predictable.

PEs will often invest in growth stages and later rounds, so your startup, if you are in the early stage, will most likely not be a fit. Wait until you are at a Series C or Series D round of financing before seeking funding from private equity.

8

Investment Rounds Explained

SECURING INVESTMENT FOR ANY STARTUP tends to occur in defined stages. These investment rounds allow startup founders to seek, attract, and then negotiate the capital they need to take their company to the next stage.

If you've just launched your first startup, then some of these investment rounds can seem confusing. Understanding each one can help you better negotiate with potential investors, and let investors know that your business knowledge is sound.

More than simply understanding the terminology and what each round entails, you'll also need to know which rounds are specific to your situation, and how to navigate each one effectively. Figure 8.1 provides a good summary of what the financing lifecycle of a startup looks like.

Let's now discuss each investment round in greater detail to help you identify investors and maximize your success rate.

Friends and Family

This preliminary round of funding is usually the first port of call for an aspiring startup entrepreneur. It's here that you raise the capital

89

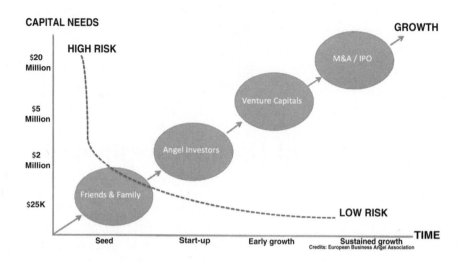

Figure 8.1   Financing Lifecycle of a Startup

Source: European Business Angel Association.

you need to get your startup off the ground, and that is done by asking friends and family to invest in your business idea.

While it is often necessary to approach family and friends for initial funding, there are situations in which you may not need their help, or would want to avoid this type of investment entirely.

What Are the Aims of a Preliminary Investment Round?

By its very nature a preliminary investment round is expected to be followed by subsequent rounds. You are not seeking enough funds to bring your project to fruition, but enough to *test the concept*.

In this circumstance, if we take an example of a smartphone app, you would need the finances to hire the software developer to create a prototype. You could then offer this prototype to a small group of consumers and test for feedback.

In essence, then, the preliminary round helps your startup create a prototype or organizational structure that will then allow you to move on and initiate subsequent investment rounds.

Your four aims during a preliminary investment round involving friends and family are:

1. **Concept development:** If you are lucky to have a fully realized concept for your product/service at this stage, that's great, but most won't. By raising a small amount of capital from friends and family, you can try a few different concepts out. This can involve artistic or technical mock-ups to develop a solid idea on which your startup company will be based.

2. **Preliminary market research:** A startup without a target marketplace is like a rudderless boat that begins taking on water: It has no direction, and it will sink fast! Initial investments can be put to good use by researching the marketplace. This can involve hiring a market research company to carry out some small surveys for you to see how well a concept would be received. It can also take the form of putting in the hours to research your product/service vision in the context of existing competition. How will your business stand out and grab the attention of consumers?

3. **Viability:** This is perhaps the most important part of this investment stage. Once your market research and product/service concept is more concrete (it could still change drastically throughout the development process), then it's time to do a financial viability study. What are the manufacturing costs? What will your running or maintenance costs be? How much investment will you need to get your product to launch? How successful will your company have to be to break even and then make a profit? How long will all of this take?

4. **Pitch development:** Another way preliminary investment can be used is for development of materials for subsequent investment rounds. Again, this could include artist mock-ups of a project, PowerPoint presentations, market research, and financial projections. These materials can then be used to

take your company into seed or series A investment (which we will discuss shortly).

Who Are Preliminary Investors?

Preliminary investors can be mostly family members or friends. These investors will help you test a concept and help your startup get on its feet so that it's a more desirable opportunity for investors.

Does My Startup Need a Preliminary Investment Round?

Preliminary investment is not always required. You may have the required capital already at your disposal, but what's more likely is that you won't need much capital to create a proof of concept. Furthermore, preliminary investment, especially when coming from family and friends, will not usually generate a large amount of capital.

It may be that you'll have to skip the preliminary round or use it in tandem with other investment rounds in order to create a viable base for your startup. (Approaching family and friends is a great option if the investment costs will be low.)

Micro Seed Round

The micro seed investment round is a model of funding that, like the preliminary round, will help get your startup on solid ground.

Where it differs, however, is that it usually involves investment from angel investors, seed venture capitalists, accelerators, incubators or crowdfunding networks across a limited time frame, rather than investment from family and friends.

What Are the Aims of a Micro Seed Investment Round?

Micro seed investment is usually available only to younger startup entrepreneurs, although that is not always the case. The purpose of this round is to provide just enough capital to allow startup founders to work full time on their project over a limited period, usually around three months. At the end of this period, founders will be expected to give a presentation to existing and potential investors, showing the viability of their product or service.

If founders can show that they have a potentially profitable business on their hands, a subsequent amount of capital will then be made available to take the project to the next phase. Micro seed investment is primarily meant to help test a concept with a conditional offer of further investment should the initial phase prove successful. It is not a *guarantee* of full investment.

The four aims of micro seed investment are:

1. **Product identification:** To attract micro seed investment, you will normally have chosen a proven marketplace to explore or a consumer need you want to meet. Seed investment will allow your startup to solidify design elements, pushing you toward a more defined product/service, and perhaps even allow you to create a prototype.

2. **Market orientation:** While you might have an idea about marketplaces you wish to explore, with micro seed investment you will be able to put some resources toward carrying out market research. This will allow you to understand the competition and how to operate more effectively within a specific niche.

3. **Demographic targeting:** Market research will not only allow you to understand the marketplace you are thinking of entering, but it will also help you to identify the target demographics most important to your niche.

4. **Team creation:** While your startup will no doubt add to its personnel during subsequent investment rounds, at the micro seed stage you should be able to put your core team into place. Startup management is often about having the right expertise working in the right roles, and with this established, your startup will be a more attractive investment opportunity in the future.

Who Are Micro Seed Investors?

Micro seed investors tend to be one of the following:

- **Angel investors:** Individuals who focus on investing at the earliest gestation stages.
- **Crowdfunding:** Third-party businesses such as Onevest that put many investors in touch with startup projects to pull resources, minimizing risks and maximizing profits.
- **Incubators:** A company that offers assistance to startup entrepreneurs such as office space, training, and management advice. This can result in seed investment and can build the foundation for a longer business arrangement.
- **Accelerators:** An investment program that provides mentorship and capital in return for equity such as Y Combinator or Techstars. This is put in place to help a startup grow over a three- to four-month period, and is therefore a shorter arrangement than that of an incubator.
- **Micro venture capitalists:** Investors who specialize in providing capital to brand new startups in a high-risk, high-rewards approach. This type of venture capitalist is a relatively new form of investor, who aims to fill the gap between the conception of a startup and more comprehensive investment.

Does My Startup Require Micro Seed Investment?

There are pros and cons of micro seed investment and they should be taken very carefully into consideration. Micro seed investment often restricts startup founders, in some cases hindering the search for investment outside of the micro seed process. That being said, it does usually only last for a few months and can be a real lifeline to some startup founders.

As with other forms of preliminary investment, initial micro seed investment covers only the very basic steps you need to take to establish your startup. It will usually not immediately provide the funds to help you get to market, although those types of funds might be made available should you show your micro seed investors that you have made good use of the original setup capital.

Seed Round

Broadly speaking, this investment round has the same function as the previous two preliminary rounds—to "seed" your startup so that it can begin to grow. However it can be distinguished from micro seed investment in a number of ways. In any case, any investment in a startup prior to a Series A round can actually be considered a seed round.

What Is Seed Investment?

Seed investment works in the same way as micro seed investment; some might even use the terms interchangeably, but it differs in two distinct ways. First of all, in terms of scale a normal seed round can be seen as a larger version of micro seed investment, although interestingly micro seed investment groups didn't come first and are relatively new, while seed investment funds have been around for a much longer time. The purpose is therefore the same, to help a startup reach its early goals.

Seed investment, however, tends to be given in larger amounts by bigger investment groups. It is seen as a high-risk type of investment, and so investors are more cautious than usual when committing themselves to this process, even more so than micro seed investment because the amount of capital at risk is much greater.

The second distinction between a seed investment round and a micro seed investment round is that a seed investment tends to be greater in scope. Most micro seed investments provide the minimum amount of funding to help a startup develop a proof of concept, and to do so over a very short time frame. The reason for this is that micro seed venture capitalists tend to invest smaller amounts of money.

A "normal" seed investment can take a startup close to market, depending on the capital requirements versus the amounts made available by seed investors. That being said, this type of investment is still preliminary, and is designed to get a startup into a position where it is strong, healthy, and ready for more investment; it is simply more robust than the other preliminary rounds.

Micro seed investment also usually requires demonstration of a prototype at the end of the three-month gestation period. With standard seed investment, your startup may not be required to do this. You may, however, be asked to have a ready design for your product/service, alongside having undertaken extensive market research to identify the markets and demographics you need to target.

You should also have your essential team in place, including management and designers, and possibly even manufacturing, advertising, and distribution personnel. From my perspective this may be the most important aspect.

Who Are Seed Investors?

Seed investors tend to be angel investors and larger seed venture capitalists that normally have under management up to $50 million in capital. They tend to be willing to invest much larger amounts than their micro seed equivalents. Seed investors take risks, and many of the investments they make may not work out, but a well-managed venture capitalist group or angel investment portfolio, for example, will still see profits due to the startups that do work out generating substantial returns.

A strategy used by seed institutional investors is the spray and pray type of model in which investment funds are invested in a number of companies and see which ones pick up traction. Once the startups they are taking on are identified, then you allocate additional capital to invest in follow-on rounds of financing. Some of the firms that operate with this model and have achieved success include 500 startups and SV Angel.

Does My Startup Need Seed Investment?

Full-scale seed investment can provide a large share of the money required to bring your product through the conceptual and prototype stages. This type of investment, however, tends to be reserved for startups that could potentially generate many millions of dollars in revenue. Only then can seed investment on this scale be justified.

Most startups will not be able to attract this level of investment and will have to approach smaller investors in order to raise the capital they need. But if your startup can genuinely show potential for generating huge revenues, then this could still be a valuable route to pursue.

In the event you do not have a good amount of revenue to showcase, you can always look into how quickly you are scaling your user base and the type of engagement that you are receiving from your users on a monthly basis. A good example of a company that has achieved great success without significant revenues is Snapchat.

Series A Round

We now come to the "series" of investment rounds. Each of these rounds serves a different function, but series A is often difficult to define, because the term is used interchangeably with preliminary and seed rounds. Here, however, we will discuss the Series A investment round as a distinct round with its own goals, investors, and advantages. Again, while some of these terms overlap, it's essential that you as a startup founder are aware of each so that you can more effectively negotiate with investors, showing that you are knowledgeable.

What Are the Aims of Series A Investment?

Series A investment is often the first investment round a startup founder will encounter in which institutional investors participate. However, even if your business has required seed investment or preliminary investment of some kind, you may still find investors referring to the following investment round as "Series A." This is often the first major form of investment a startup will secure.

As the name implies, this investment round is often followed by others, and so, just like preliminary rounds, it is not usually considered as the last investment round a startup will require, but it's the stage of investment that will allow your company to launch its product/service.

This form of investment is often given through preferred stock, which is a form of fixed dividend given to investors, which provides them with a priority over subsequent investors. This means that if there are acquisition holders of preferred stock, they will be able to sell their shares before common stockholders.

This may not be so important in the event the company does a good exit over the last round's valuation. However, in the event the company is sold for an amount that is below the valuation in which investors invested, then preferred stock is particularly important as they might be able to recover some of their losses while common stockholders may be left holding the bag.

The four goals for this stage of investment include:

1. **Distribution:** Establishing advertising strategies and the most effective ways to disseminate information about your product, service, or brand is a key part of Series A investment. By achieving distribution channels for both marketing and product delivery, your startup can lower costs and increase sales.
2. **New markets:** Series A investment is often sought by startup founders in order to move into new marketplaces through the injection of capital, engaging with different demographics, and furthering brand visibility in the process.
3. **Next level:** At this stage your business may be established, so Series A investment can be seen as a way to take your startup to the next phase of your business plan. This could take the form of a new product or service, or it could be improving manufacturing or organizational aspects of your business to help improve profits.
4. **Shortfall:** Your startup may be a promising investment opportunity, but it could be that due to unforeseen events

it lacks the cash to become fully self-sufficient. Series A investment can provide the financial resources to achieve just that.

Who Are Series A Investors?

Series A investors are usually venture capitalists or angels. If taking place after a seed round of investment, potential series A investors will evaluate how any seed capital was used and whether this would bode well for their capital. Other profiles of investors that may participate in these types of rounds include family offices, private equity firms, hedge funds, and corporate venture arms.

Do I Need Series A Investment?

This investment round is usually entered into when two needs are satisfied.

First of all, you must have a clearly defined product/service that you hope to produce. Second, you will have the correct infrastructure in place to reach your business goals with subsequent investment.

If your company is running out of capital to bring a product to market, the series A investment is a great avenue to help launch your product/service. Otherwise, you can do what people call a "bridge round," which is an extension of your seed round in order to buy you additional time to hit milestones that would help you land the Series A round.

Series B, C, D Investment Rounds

Strictly speaking, other than an IPO, most subsequent forms of investment will be alphabetized. Each series will have a specific goal, but that will be defined by you, the startup founder, and existing investors based on what your company needs.

Series B investment, for example, is usually entered into once your product/service is launched and more capital is needed to expand profits and market share. In essence, series B investment helps a company scale up their operations to take the business onto the next level. This could be entering into a new marketplace or increasing advertising. This is often easier than series A investment and has a smaller amount of risk attached to it because your product/service is already established. For this reason, it is common for series B investment to be larger than series A.

Moreover, you would be raising a Series B round in the event you want to start expanding overseas and need to either hire staff or acquire a local company in order to achieve the rapid growth that you want to obtain.

Series C investment and beyond is usually sought after when a startup needs to expand further or is getting ready for a major acquisition. This is usually the last stage before an IPO, but as stated previously, series D investment rounds (and further down the alphabet) are not unheard of.

Most series investment will be offered by venture capitalists or investment funds.

Initial Public Offering (IPO)

The initial public offering (IPO) round is not entered into until a startup has entered into a well-established stage. This is a standard route that many companies take to generate new investment because it can be extremely effective.

It normally takes a good amount of time to get to an IPO. For example, Facebook did its IPO in 2012 after eight years of being in operations. Google, for example, was registered as a domain in 1997 and the company went public in 2004.

What Is an IPO Investment Round?

An IPO is the first step to opening your company up to public investment. Up until this point your startup will have relied on a combination of personal funds and angel investors, venture capital, seed money, and series investors—but now you are offering a percentage of your company to anyone who is willing to legally invest capital.

This is a straightforward equity for capital swap and is offered via shares/stocks. If someone owns 28 percent of shares, they technically own the same percentage of the company, minus any protected portion.

Each time that shares are released during an IPO event, the shares that current investors hold are diluted slightly, unless there is an antidilution agreement in place to protect against loss of share value.

Who Are IPO Investors?

The fact that an IPO is a public event means that anyone can invest, as long as they can afford the current share price. Some investors will buy directly, while others will have their advisors or fund managers make the buying and selling decisions for them. Often your shareholders will be those with an investment history, or those interested in the marketplace and industry you are entering.

Should I Take My Company Public?

Broadly speaking there are two main reasons for a startup founder to provide an IPO for their company. The first is that it's an extremely reliable, quick way to raise capital. If your startup requires additional funds to continue as is, or to develop new revenue streams via products and untapped marketplaces, an IPO is a great option.

Another reason for initiating an IPO is that you and/or major investors are holding onto restricted stock. These shares have stringent legal stipulations attached to them, which have usually been agreed upon during previous investment rounds. It could be that you are not allowed to sell your stock for a specific amount of time, or to others, without offering it to your investors first. You may not want to sell your shares, which could allow a specific investor to have more influence over your company.

More than likely, however, the reason your existing stock will be restricted and deemed "unsellable" is that it hasn't been technically verified by the government. Without an IPO, you may not be able to legally sell your stock unless it is during a liquidity event, when you'd be able to convert your stock into cash.

In other words, an IPO not only brings capital into your business, but if you want to sell your stock in the company at a later date, you'll need to carry out an IPO so that your stock can be legally validated.

Take caution—an IPO is not always desirable. It can infer that a company is having difficulties with cash flow. It can also be the case that your product, service, or brand is simply not desirable yet and therefore your shares either don't sell, or they plummet along with the standing of your startup. This can be a disaster if your IPO is your exit strategy.

Only enter into such an investment round when you are convinced your company is ready to go public and reap the financial rewards. Remember that when you go public there are a lot of reporting and compliance regulations that you need to follow. The Securities and Exchange Commission is very protective where small investors are concerned.

Research Is Critical

A lot of ground has been covered in this chapter, but you should now have a firmer grasp of the types of investment rounds best suited to your needs, and have a better understanding of how to navigate them to your advantage.

9

Deciding Investment Amounts and Prospects

Now that we understand the various investment rounds that you will encounter throughout the development of your startup, it's important to have a strategy for how to identify and engage with prospects, as well as a realistic concept of how much to ask from investors.

Needed, Realistic, and Ideal Investment Levels

Before we identify prospective investors, you should implicitly understand the differences between needed, realistic, and ideal investments. You should develop a separate costing outline for each, allowing you to understand what your company needs to launch, survive, grow, and return a profit for you and your investors. It will also provide you with a clearer way to identify needed, realistic, and ideal investors during the negotiation process, leading to a strong valuation of your startup.

- **Ideal investment:** This investment level is the best-case scenario. This level of investment that will allow you to put in place all of your infrastructure as well as covering all manufacturing, distribution, and advertising costs. Not only that, but an ideal investment will provide enough capital to cover all costs and provide your startup with a substantial reserve for future expansion. Gaining ideal investment straightaway, if at all, is very rare, but defining the perfect scenario will help to create a good project roadmap.

- **Needed investment:** This is the investment amount you require to meet your startup's immediate goals. Those goals will be determined by what combination of investment rounds you are pursuing. If, for example, you are looking for seed investment, then the immediate needs for your company will include market research, conceptual design, developing infrastructure, and creating a prototype. Needed investment will allow you to achieve the absolute minimum to push your startup forward. Knowing how much capital is required to keep your startup developing as a going concern is imperative.

- **Realistic investment:** This investment level is based on how much capital you can expect to raise overall, and how much you can expect to raise for each investor. The types of investors you are hoping to attract will answer the latter. If you are raising capital from friends and family, their financial situation will define how much they can invest. An individual angel investor is probably going to contribute a smaller amount than a VC group. Whoever your target investor is, you need to be realistic about how much capital to expect from them. A "realistic" investment is a much more subjective number than are "needed" and "ideal" figures, but it will give you an investment amount to aim for, and should be closer to any compromise at the conclusion of negotiations.

Knowing the difference between realistic, needed, and ideal investment levels for your business will help you chart a course through each investment round, informing your negotiation decisions in terms of how much capital you need to develop your startup to different levels within best- to worst-case scenario time frames.

From my experience in raising capital, it is important to understand how much it will take to oversubscribe the round quickly, and whether you have the people whom you can tap for capital. Once you have a clear understanding of who will invest (for certain), then determine a round amount. Normally, when you are oversubscribed, the story becomes more attractive and your round is much easier to sell.

Your Valuation versus Market Valuation: The Asking Price

Now that you know what you need, you should focus on the valuation of your startup. This simply refers to how much equity you should give investors in return for their capital.

In essence there are two types of valuation that you will encounter:

- **Founder valuation:** How much you believe your business is worth.
- **Market valuation:** This type of valuation is essentially how much your business is worth to investors when taking into consideration investment risks. In other words, your startup is worth what someone is willing to pay for it.

Both types of valuation will usually contradict each other. This difference in agreement is where negotiation of terms takes place. In the end, the agreed-upon valuation of your business will depend on the following nine factors:

1. How much money you need to achieve your goals
2. The type of investor (angel, VC, family and friends, etc.)
3. Your prior success as an entrepreneur
4. The "going rate" for similar companies (comparables)
5. The growth rate of related sectors/marketplaces

6. How likely it is that your startup will reach profitability
7. The level of revenue currently or potentially generated by the business
8. The team that you have around you
9. Customer acquisition and distribution of your company

In essence, your job as a startup founder is to persuade investors that your business is worth a certain amount. The valuation of your startup is a fluid, subjective figure; for that reason, it is best to have a minimum and maximum range in mind rather than a single number. This will give you more room to negotiate.

The best way to show investors that your startup is worth your valuation is to have a well-structured business plan and have as much market research in place as possible, as well as a financial forecast (which I will cover shortly).

You definitely do not want to price your company too high or you will scare people off. You will need to research the market and ask around about valuations that some of your direct or indirect competitors had when they were raising money at your same stage. This type of data will be very useful, and information that you can also leverage during the negotiation process with investors.

Persuading Investors with a Financial Forecast

If you want to attract investment, then you have to show why your startup is an opportunity that they wouldn't want to miss. To do this you will be required to present some kind of forecast to potential investors.

When it comes to startups it is very difficult to know where you will be in five years. Who would have thought in 2004 that Facebook would be valued at $100 billion in 2012? The forecast is your most effective persuasive tool, but it is also one of the most difficult to compile. Financial forecasts predict where a business will be per quarter, per trading year. (As I've already discussed, your timeline to reach the breakeven point should be concrete when it's included.)

Your forecast should outline the following for investors:

■ Projected income
■ Estimated expenses
■ Expected growth

A financial forecast should not be confused with a business plan. It is a carefully constructed projection of company development over a given time period, taking into consideration projected sales data, as well as market and economic indicators.

Normally you would want to include at least three years so that the investor can see the key drivers of your business over the course of time. Some investors may want up to five years, but in my opinion, that's too much.

You will need someone who is very good with numbers to nail the forecast. In my case, I had our CFO very close to me when developing our forecast. Barry Shereck has taken four companies public as a CFO, so I knew I had guidance from the best, and you should take the time to make sure you have the best possible help, too, if forecasting is not your strength.

For potential investors, a strong financial forecast will help with the following five factors:

1. Show the financial viability of your startup as a new business
2. Identify potential risks that could affect business cash flow
3. Provide a clear understanding of future financial needs, including if subsequent investment will be required
4. Allow future comparisons between forecast and business operations so that startup management can adjust the business to reach estimated goals
5. Show financial responsibility on the part of the founder

Your financial forecast is not only a critical tool to attract investment, but it will help you to show more clearly why you value your startup at a specific figure. If you can show reliably that the business should generate healthy revenue, then investors will be more likely to accept less equity in return for the same level of capital investment.

Ultimately your forecast will help the investor see how the money that is being raised will be put to use and the impact it will have on the long-term plans of the company. As I mentioned previously, it is all about speeding up the machine, and the forecast should show how the new money will accelerate things down the line.

Identifying Prospective Investors

In the sales world, we talk about "prospects." A prospect is an individual or organization that can be considered a prospective buyer; in other words, anyone a business should contact to sell a product to because they are more likely to make a specific purchasing decision than others. Seeking investment is a similar process. Your potential investors should still be considered as prospects.

Not everyone is a potential investor, and it's important that you don't waste your time and resources chasing every single lead. Only a few will be genuine prospects, and it's up to you to decide who is and who isn't. A good potential investor should have the following qualities:

- Interest in the sector your startup will be trading in
- The prospect has the necessary capital to contribute to your startup's immediate needs
- The prospect will listen to your pitch
- The prospect is reliable and has a trustworthy reputation
- They understand entrepreneurship and have a decent level of business acumen.

As a founder, you need to use these qualities as a benchmark, and a profile, which will allow you to more readily identify the right investors.

There are great tools available to search for potential prospects, such as Crunchbase, where you search for competitors' profiles and discover who invested in them. And with tools like LinkedIn you can find out who you have in common with specific investors, and connect to make an introduction.

Create an Excel sheet that lets you keep track of every conversation you are in with investors at all points in the process. This way you know when to follow up and how.

Six Ways to Contact Investors

Identifying the type of individual who will be a potential investor is only half the battle. It is up to you as a startup entrepreneur to be proactive and search for potential investors who fit your investor profile.

Here are six effective ways to source and contact your prospective investors:

1. **LinkedIn:** This professional social media site is a must for contemporary entrepreneurs. It showcases who you are, your business interests, and your career portfolio. What's more, it puts you directly in contact with those involved in similar industries. Over time, your "network" will increase, and with it, a list of potential investors to contact. A premium account is a must, and while there is a small outlay, it will increase your visibility to investors and increase your ability to search for individuals you think might be interested in your project. If you already have a LinkedIn account, go through your network and draw up a list of prospects—those who you believe can either provide capital for your business, or connections that your startup will benefit from.

2. **Customers:** Do you already have potential customers interested in your startup product/service? If so, they may be willing to take things one step further and invest in your business. This includes any customers from other businesses

you are involved in, if any. (You'll be surprised how many people are willing to invest small amounts of capital in businesses producing products that are of interest to them.)

3. **Fans:** If you've been promoting the concept of your startup online, you've likely already attracted a group of people who are interested in what you are offering. While they might not have intimated that they will buy your products or service, they may be open to investing.

4. **Advisors:** It's rare for any entrepreneur to establish him- or herself without receiving a little help, even if it comes in the form of advice. Who has been advising you? Have you spoken to established businesses? Do you have any mentors? There's a good chance that if you have been advised by individuals with investment capital, they will invest in your project.

5. **Events:** If you are going to compete within an industry, you have to be part of it. Research upcoming events related to your business and attend them as often as possible. Conferences, conventions, and so forth can be excellent places to meet potential investors and help expand your network.

6. **Crowdsourcing:** By using a service such as Onevest, you can place your startup in the shop window and let investors come to you. Crowdsourcing is a fantastic way to attract investment quickly.

For investors, time is their best friend, and it lets them understand your execution and level of performance. It also reduces, to a certain degree, the risk of their investment if all the boxes are checked.

Unfortunately, for entrepreneurs, time is often their worst enemy. Entrepreneurs need to move very quickly when raising money, because prospects can disappear.

You can keep your business fresh in prospects' minds when time is tight by writing a blog post or sending a newsletter to your community with updates on your fundraising progress.

Creating a Buzz around Your Startup

Now that we've discussed the process of deciding on investment amounts and identifying prospects, we can move on to creating momentum for your startup, and promoting your business as a golden opportunity for investors.

10

PR: Creating a Storm and Building Momentum

PR IS A PIVOTAL PART of both fundraising and overall startup success. Done right, PR is the ultimate guerrilla warfare tool for startups. Executed poorly, it can cost you the movement you need.

How do you create the storm that propels your fundraising efforts, and your startup's valuation potential?

The Rainmaker Code

There are three keys to successfully creating a PR storm that can bring the funding your startup needs:

1. Timing
2. Synergy
3. Efficiency

Timing

Timing is critical for startups, but often not for the reasons entrepreneurs think. Too many are consumed with the hunger to be noticed and succeed overnight. But for those who are focused, it's actually easy to make a massive PR splash without straining your cash stores. Show some know-how and smart creativity—many serious investors love being among the first to know about and jump in on a savvy investment opportunity.

Synergy

All PR has to have synergy, with a mapped out fundraising and growth plan, and your communications have to sing the heart of the brand. Make sure all PR is woven with your messaging and branding, and will resonate with your prospective investors and early adopters. Proper planning includes being seen in the right places, being mentioned by the right people, and in the right contexts.

Efficiency

Although getting noticed and gaining steam are critical parts of fundraising and business growth, both have to be done efficiently and cost effectively. Looking too cheap or coming across as too extravagant (or far worse, careless) can both be equally destructive. Your PR efforts have to deliver results and value, and the outcomes have to be fully capitalized on.

Journalist Outreach

Connecting with journalists is one of the most common first outreach methods many startup entrepreneurs attempt. This can be valuable, but it is often executed so poorly that it can go beyond counterproductive to almost self-sabotaging.

Journalists can be a great help in your quest for funding, but the problem lies in the effectiveness of the approach that entrepreneurs use. If you haven't run into it yet, you'll find that most available lists of journalists' contact information are usually out of date, which equates to spinning wheels and wasted time. Even if journalists are reachable, there can be even more time spent pitching stories, conducting interviews, and following up, without any promise of results.

Local journalists are often easiest to reach and connect with, and can be allies for your business. News about people and companies that can benefit the local economy are a win-win for all involved parties. Find journalists in your town, city, and/or state by scouting local publications, or LinkedIn.

Local publications that create their own press releases have ties with distribution services that will blast out stories and recommend them to thousands of journalists. Going local can be the most cost- and time-effective route in most cases.

Six Hacks for Effective Journalist Outreach

1. Focus on inbound-outbound warm blogger outreach
2. Try HARO (help a reporter out; www.helpareporter.com)
3. Use Publiseek
4. Tap local press connections
5. Choose a press release service that includes blasts to journalists
6. Follow reporters on Twitter and engage with their tweets so they start recognizing who you are

Bloggers are the grassroots cogs that are responsible for a lot of buzz, visibility, and traction today. One of the best ways to reach and leverage them is by being useful to them. Be their solution. Bloggers need fresh content every day. They live on great new stories and leads.

By running your own startup blog and posting shareable and quotable content, you can become a top go-to resource in your industry or niche. Consider publishing new infographics, then emailing key bloggers to encourage them to share them.

Your content could also be a great resource in terms of customer acquisition. Mint (mint.com) found success before their acquisition in part by posting great content that captivated the attention of prospective customers. Search engines also love great content. When you write engaging content with a wide range of descriptive words, this can enable your site to show up in search results when potential investors search for keywords related to your industry.

HARO and Publiseek offer channels for connecting with journalists and publications that are actively seeking stories like yours, or looking for experts like you for commentary. Recently, Publiseek transitioned from a free service to one that charges per-service fees (which you may consider expensive, depending on your budget). HARO appears to have moved in the opposite direction, with a low monthly subscription fee.

Self-Distributed Press Releases

The media today is incredibly malleable. We no longer live in a time when a few authoritative publications and journalists present the news with well-researched, high-quality information. In the 21st century, for better or worse, anyone can generate news.

If you've ever been frustrated by a competitor's media mentions, coverage, or praise, the new reality may be comforting. It means you can hold a position in media coverage as well. In this era of multiple channels, soundbites, and heavy editing, achieving attention often isn't about being the best—it's about knowing how to use the system.

I want to be clear—not being a media expert is no excuse not to strive for excellence, no matter what you've chosen to contribute to the world. But do work with the knowledge that the arena has changed.

Much of what we read today is the self-published content of brands, organizations, and entrepreneurs seeking to get their messages across. There is nothing wrong with this, but making your way through the crowd of voices and messages (all at varying levels of quality and persistence) can be a challenge.

So how do you get featured in the news as the expert, the next rising super startup to invest in, or must-have trending product or service? There are now several ways to hack the press, including:

- Press release distribution services
- Submitting your releases and stories to local newspapers
- Paying for specific publication placement for advertorials and sponsored stories

Regular inclusion in local media often depends on building direct relationships, which can either be a gold mine, or a time-consuming maze.

Sponsored stories can be incredibly powerful. This is especially true when they land in highly authoritative niche publications. But, startups and entrepreneurs need to be realistic about the expectations for results and costs.

For example, it is highly unlikely that you are going to land a spot in *Venture Beat* or the *Huffington Post* for $50. Some publications charge thousands of dollars to include a single story. At Facebook, it's one of their main revenue streams, although Facebook marketing is available at a tiny fraction of the cost.

There are now multiple services that will circulate your self-generated press release for a modest fee. These include:

- OnlinePRNews
- PRNewswire
- PRWeb
- PRLog
- 24–7 Press Release
- Business Wire

Some of these services are free, or have free options. Expect that you'll get what you pay for. It can be worth testing out different platforms and press release packages in order to maximize your reach and ROI.

According to *Forbes*, press releases are a vital form of authentic content.[1] They carry many benefits. Beyond heightened visibility this means positioning, credibility, viral potential, funneling web traffic, and SEO (search engine optimization) for boosting Google rankings.

Note that in 2015 Google restored the value it puts on online press releases after taking a break due to overuse.

Best Practices for Creating Your Own Press Releases

- Make sure they are professionally written (hire a freelance writer if you need to)
- Make them newsworthy
- Ensure they are relevant to current trends and conversation
- Include well-researched keywords
- Include backlinks to your online assets (include only one for every 300 words, or you will be labeled as spam by search engines)
- Add social media feeds, images, and iFrames of your website where possible
- Make sure to time your release for optimal pickup and circulation
- Don't just swing and hope—distribute with purpose

Ten Things to Publish in a Press Release

1. The coming launch of your product or service
2. Casting calls for early adopters
3. Announcing the closing of a round of funding
4. Announcing a new round of funding (comply with general solicitation and Title II of the JOBS Act)
5. Raising awareness of a crowdfunding campaign
6. Highlighting notable additions to your development or executive team, or board members
7. Live events
8. Your founding story

---

[1] http://www.forbes.com/sites/jaysondemers/2014/12/29/where-press-releases-fit-in-your-2015-seo-strategy/.

9. Accomplishment of major milestones
10. How your product or service is solving a trending need

How to Maximize Your PR ROI

Startups must be intentional if they want to really get value out of their PR. Otherwise, it is like shouting in the woods, or putting up a lavish billboard with no phone number, website address, or logo. You must clearly identify your objectives, create a funnel to facilitate them, and follow through.

So what are the tangible objectives that you'll design your PR to accomplish? What specific outcomes will determine whether it is a success, or not? Is it landing a specific amount of funding? Generating a certain number of new adopters or website hits? Is it simply getting picked up by 12 credible news sites? How about generating additional press interviews and boosting your website's Google search ranking?

Whatever your PR goals and vehicles are, make sure that there are clear calls to action in place, and a streamlined funnel. For example, add a call for more interviews and a phone number, a targeted landing page link and URL for pre-orders, or links to your crowdfunding campaign page. Make sure you track and measure all of these factors, too. This way they can be evaluated, ROI can be effectively tracked, and future PR can be maximized.

In any case, investors love press mentions and it will make them see that your company is gaining traction and attention from the public. This ends up increasing your mindshare and also the value of your business.

More Buzz-Building Tactics for Smart Startups

Partnerships and Business Development Deals

PR can be a great tool for forging new partnerships and business development deals, and vice versa. Make some noise when you land a notable partner or distribution channel. In turn, leverage these partners and their resources to generate even more PR. They ought to have existing connections and be engaging in regular media opportunities. You may even make this a part of your conversations before tying the knot.

Month-over-Month Growth

Consistent month-over-month growth is critical for startups. It ensures they stay on the right track. It not only keeps existing investors happy and increases the odds that they'll make follow-up investments, but helps to attract new investors as well. Some may choose to sit on the sidelines and see how you perform for a little while. This is especially true of VCs. They want to see that you have the grit to stick it out, that there is demand for your product or service, that you can be profitable without funding, and that you know how to run a tight ship. So press releases can be a great tool for highlighting your growth track record. At the same time, press releases and similar tools can be used to spur that growth.

If you look deeply into the growth patterns of other notable startups that have attracted major funding or have even already gone to an IPO, you'll discover many plateaus, not straight-line growth. Press releases and other marketing pushes and spurts can be essential for breaking through these ceilings and vaulting to the next level of users, revenues, and funding.

Product Launches and Events

PR tools like press releases are ideal for maximizing events, including product launches. Build up the excitement in advance to ensure strong attendance and success. Use them to beef up overall attendance numbers, as well as specifically attracting investors and local and national press journalists. This applies to online launches as well as pop-up events and panels.

Don't overlook the power of sponsorships, either. PR can be used to recruit more sponsors to offset the expense of organizing and hosting an event. Or perhaps you are at the stage where sponsoring or providing your product or service to another event host can boost visibility, generate free press coverage, and get your startup in front of key investors in a warm way.

Social Media and Blogging

Social media and blogging can become the epicenter of your PR campaign, and the tools to maximize the coverage you generate. With blogging as the heart of your venture you can simultaneously build up an online presence and develop SEO that you own and control. This provides long-term marketing benefits. Furthermore, you can splice off blog content and spread it via social media. This can be key blog content, infographics, video, statistics and market updates, news items, or competitions. Then push this content out to journalists and editors. Be sure to complete the loop by mentioning any pick-ups you get on your blog and social media profiles. If you generate results for those who pick you up, they'll keep coming back for more, and essentially become long-term partners in driving your success.

Ultimately PR is a key component in both fundraising and the long-term success of a startup. Press releases are a powerful part of PR strategy. There are many ways to enhance their benefits within your full PR plan, and results must be built into original plans and budgeting.

11

What to Look For in an Investor

WE'VE ALREADY COVERED WAYS TO find prospective investors and how to convert them. But entrepreneurs who are serious about their startups know that not just any investor or capital source will do.

What should you be looking for in an investor? How do you hone in quickly on the best investors and stand out as a great match?

Three Keys to Landing the Best Investors

1. Know who you do (and don't) want as an investor
2. Know how to screen an investor
3. Know how to converse with investors effectively and efficiently

Why Selecting the Right Investors Is So Critical

When you onboard an investor, that institution or individual becomes part of your cap table, and they are in for the long run. It is well known that divorcing your wife or husband is much easier than divorcing your investor. You need to be very careful with whom you are getting into bed.

Seeking the right investors is critical to get right, even for the smallest amounts of initial seed funding from friends and family. Just ask Mark Zuckerberg. And those initial investors are going to have a huge impact on who you will be able to attract for additional rounds of funding, and what those terms will be. So even if you are borrowing only $1,000 from a relative or classmate, make sure there is no lack of clarity on the agreement and that you aren't setting yourself up for heartbreak later on.

Deciding what's important in an investor or capital source at the outset helps founders streamline the process of filtering and screening, while empowering them to make good decisions. This really has little to do with the money part of the equation.

Three Factors You Should Be Looking For in Investors

Factor 1: Domain Experts

More money can be great, but there are a variety of places to get it. Don't just settle for money. Look at what else an investor can add. If you've ever watched an episode of *The Profit* with serial investor Marcus Lemonis, you've witnessed how an expert with a fresh perspective can add a ton of value.

This doesn't mean investors are going to come in and take over your business. But perhaps they can lend their experience to help you make traction. Sometimes all it takes is a few tweaks you hadn't thought of. What's offered could be business-related in general, industry-specific expertise, or simply funding and the financial aspects of your venture.

Ask what expertise this capital source brings to the table that makes him or her more valuable to you than the next one in line.

Factor 2: Connected

Look for well-connected investors. Great connections are some of the best value that you can ask for as a startup. If you can get money and connections together, that's a two-for-one not to be passed up.

Trust and power with the best connections can take years and an incredible investment to develop. Investors are guarded well, and for good reason. Yet, sometimes all it takes is the right connection for a startup to go really huge, really fast. Take any of the investors on the panel of the reality TV show *Shark Tank*, put a product or service into their hands that they can promote through their channels, and it can be an overnight hit.

It's the same concept as celebrity sponsorships. If the right celebrity is out there touting, advertising, and recommending your product to the right demographic, business can explode. Of course, most fledgling startups can't afford celebrity sponsorships like Nike or adidas, at least not in a sustainable way.

Raising capital from a connected investor flips this equation. You effectively get paid to get promoted. This isn't just about celebrity product placement or celebrity tweaks—it can mean incredibly powerful retail distribution channels, too.

Factor 3: Financial Strength

When was the last time the prospective investor funded something? How much does the investor have left? How are the investor's other investments performing? How strong is the investor financially? You don't want your startup to be the only hope for the investor.

If the investor isn't doing well financially, that person is going to be under a lot of stress, and that pressure will flow down to you. Even if it isn't that serious, it is clearly more efficient and profitable to have an investor partner who is able to provide further rounds of funding on his or her own. It is even better if they are connected to others with capital. Birds of a feather flock together.

At the other end of the spectrum, when you see a venture capital firm that has not made new investments or followed up on investments in a period of six months, you know they are running out of capital on their fund and they are having troubles in securing the next fund. Investors need to schedule regular meetings with entrepreneurs, regardless of being in investment mode or not. For this reason save yourself time and move on to another firm that has the ammunition to pull the trigger.

Three Factors to Avoid in Investors

Factor 1: Greed

There is a distinct difference between conducting a profitable business and being greedy. You can be a very successful and wealthy investor without having to be greedy. If all your investors want to do is take, take, take, and milk every dime from your startup, then your successes are not going to be sustainable or even enjoyable.

An investor may very well be able to rush you to an IPO, but that doesn't mean it will end well. Selling out your startup's soul isn't going to feel good if it is something you really care about. Even if all you care about is the money, someone who wants only to take will find every opportunity to do so. And don't forget that if you plan to move on to additional business ventures, this one is going to be at the top of your resume. It's your calling card. Even if it wasn't your vote, your startup will tell others a lot about you. What will it tell them?

You will start to see some red flags concerning this type of behavior when you are in the negotiation process of your deal. Keep your eyes open for the addition of certain clauses that are out of market. This will tell you what type of individual you are dealing with. If this person is showing these signs at the "dating" stage, imagine how things could turn out if the company is not doing well.

Factor 2: Lack of Scruples

Greed is one thing, but unscrupulous, shady individuals take things to a whole new level. If you risk colluding with people who have no values, there is really no telling how ugly it can become. And when you get even a little bit dirty it can lead to a rapid downward spiral. You can be damaged simply by association.

If there is any bad business in motion, the investor is normally going to be better insulated than the entrepreneur, leaving the founders who have their hands on the controls as easy scapegoats. This can clearly get really scary when it comes to health-care and financial startups.

No industry is off the hook. And partnerships go both ways. Savvy investors with values should be looking for good qualities in founders, too, though it isn't always easy to discern who's ethical. Take Mark Cuban's investment in Motionloft as an example. The original founder ended up being hunted by the FBI for allegedly spinning tales of a secret deal to cash in on the company while taking money from individuals. That founder naturally lost his job, and the press coverage added additional pain. If your instincts tell you something isn't right, steer clear. A bad decision can follow you forever.

Factor 3: The Takeover

If you know Steve Jobs's story, you can probably empathize with the heartache and frustration of being booted from your own startup. Few entrepreneurs get as far as being funded unless they are really passionate about their startups.

Even if you don't have the burning passion for perfection that led to the iPod, who wants all of the blood, sweat, and tears to end with getting kicked out of your own venture right before it blossoms? Getting bought out and staying on as an executive, or giving up a piece of the pie in exchange for being able to make your vision become a reality, doesn't have to be all bad.

If Facebook or Google buys in, gives you an amazing suite on their campus, and puts their teams of developers at your beck and call, it could be a dream come true. But no one wants someone else to turn his or her venture into something different and end up being relegated to the position of a powerless pawn—or worse, shut out altogether. So watch out for term requests that appear to suggest that this may be the intention.

Six Key Questions to Ask Potential Investors

Dig in and get a better feel for the real spirit and value of your potential investors quickly by knowing what questions to ask.

1. What additional expertise can this investor bring to the table?
2. Who can this investor introduce and connect me to?
3. How solvent and flush is this investor?
4. Is this investor looking to create shared success, or just take all they can?
5. Do we share the same values and level of integrity?
6. Are they asking for a large stock option pool? (This could suggest intentions to replace you.)

Speed Is a Two-Way Street

If you want to get funded fast, you have to be ready to move quickly—knowing what you want, having all of your collateral in order, and knowing how to screen investors in advance. And you need to work with investors that are going to move swiftly too. They should know the answers to your questions, how to express and convey their value, and evaluate if your venture is the right fit quickly. Again, it's a two-way street.

If one side is bogged down in overanalyzing, and gets stuck in analysis paralysis when it is time to hit the gas, that doesn't serve either driver well. Absolutely, do your due diligence in a reasonable period of time, but the moment to tune up your engine is before you hit the road. The same goes for investors. You wouldn't want to work with an angel who woke up one morning and said *"I want to invest some money,"* and then stalled you for weeks or months trying to figure out his own mechanics.

So have your documentation correct and ready, establish internal agreement between cofounders or board members, and be ready to act. At the same time watch out for signs of slow investors. How many deals have they funded recently? When was the last time they funded an enterprise? What is their close rate?

Knowing the questions to ask is a part of this. So is having screening questions ready—such as about the size of their investment—so that you aren't wasting time talking to the wrong people . . . or wasting their time, either. You'll also want to be prepared to answer the questions prospective investors will have at this stage.

Arming Yourself with Answers

For the most part, investors are going to ask you the same questions. So have your answers ready. (As you interact with an investor, be aware of his or her responses for your own benefit, as well.)

Expect to be asked:

- What is the difference between you and your primary competitors?
- When will you break even?
- How much is revenue forecast to be this year, and next year?
- How will you use the money?
- What risk factors does your business face?
- What round of funding is this for your startup?
- What terms are you seeking?
- Who is the management team, and what is their experience?
- What is your burn rate?
- Why did you start it?
- How long have you been working on this startup?
- How does the business model work?
- Do you have wider expansion plans; where and when?
- Do you hold any patents or proprietary technology?
- What makes you think you can excel in this space?
- Who are your other investors?
- How are existing investors involved?
- Are existing investors involved in this funding round?
- What's the exit strategy?
- When do you expect an exit?
- How much money has been raised so far?

Don't expect only these questions. Be prepared not only to answer the questions, but to master answering them. Creating a write-up can be a smart decision. You may not be able to include every question and answer in your pitch deck or executive summary, but you can have a document that shows authority and streamlines the early stages of the interview process for you and the investor. This also irons out bumps in the road in advance, leaps objections, and prevents stalling negotiations. You don't want to let the perfect investor slip away when she has the chance to run into another startup that is prepared—that investor will fund them with her cash instead of you. When you're fully prepared you can focus on building rapport and getting to an agreement fast.

You really don't have to (or want to) be speaking in fundraising mode the entire time you interact with a potential investor. You don't want to come across as desperate. An investor might prefer to check the boxes and spend the rest of the time talking about football or vacationing, or ideas for taking your startup to a whole new level. And you really want an investor that you can get along with. You want him or her to be on point when it comes to business, but you'll enjoy the relationship a lot more if the investor is someone you could invite to a ballgame, to a new restaurant, to go running, or to simply hang out with over a craft beer on a Friday evening.

Get to know one another on a personal level. Ask the investor about his or her family, find out about his or her favorite hobbies, and so on. From there, you can give a quick elevator pitch (not the entire story). Once you have done that, let the investor drive the conversation so that he or she is engaged at all times and connected to you. If during the meeting you do not know the answer to a question, don't be afraid to say that you don't know. Tell the investor you will do the necessary research and you will follow-up via email with the answer. You want to make sure that you leave meetings with all the questions answered and any concerns cleared up.

12

Term Sheets and Terms

THIS IS WHERE THE RUBBER meets the road on the path to getting funded. You've put in the work to prepare your startup to be fundable, you've gained intelligence on the process and who you want to invest, you've polished and flexed your pitch, and you've gained some investor interest. Now it's time to nail down the terms.

Term sheets can be really scary for new startup founders. More than anything, it's the fear of the unknown, or of making a mistake that founders may regret later, as the business grows. Term sheets are important, and can be complex, but they don't necessarily have to be. The key is knowing what to expect, knowing what you want out of a term sheet, knowing what you won't bend to, and of course having good representation to review all of the fine print.

So what is in a term sheet? What don't you want to see in your term sheets? What strategies may help founders get more of what they want?

Term Sheets 101

The term sheet is the document that lays out the terms of the investment and collateral. It details what you as the startup are giving, and what you are getting in return. Then it lays out the guidelines of how both parties will act to protect the investment.

Term sheets can vary depending on what type of funding round you are in, and how much is at stake, as well as who is involved. Generally term sheets for seed rounds are going to be much lighter and shorter than for series A or beyond. The less at stake, the less complex it should be, as no one wants to unnecessarily splurge on extra legal fees, or burning time. The process can be significantly simplified when using a third-party funding portal.

In a seed round, the investor will typically be the one providing the term sheet. This may change, especially when there are multiple investors in later and larger rounds.

What's in a term sheet? Common items in a term sheet include:

- Who is issuing the note or stock
- Type of collateral being offered
- The valuation
- Amount being offered
- Shares and price
- What happens on liquidation or IPO
- Voting rights
- Board seats
- Conversion options
- Antidilution provisions
- Investors rights to information
- Founders obligations
- Who will pay legal expenses
- Nondisclosure requirements
- Rights to future investment
- Signatures

A term sheet might just be one page or it could be 10 pages long. Generally speaking, simplicity is often preferred by founders, but it pays to have clarity and make sure all bases are covered. An example of a term sheet is shown in the following box, but you will need to have great counsel guiding you through the process and providing the right materials. This sample is only for your information.

Term Sheet

Series A Preferred Stock Financing of [Name of Company]

This Term Sheet summarizes the principal terms of the Series A Preferred Stock Financing of [NAME OF COMPANY] a [NAME STATE] corporation (the "**Company**"). No legally binding obligations will be created until definitive agreements are executed and delivered by all parties. This Term Sheet is not a commitment to invest, and is conditioned on the completion of due diligence, legal review, and documentation that is satisfactory to the Investors. This Term Sheet shall be governed in all respects by the laws of [NAME STATE].

Offering Terms
Company:
Securities:
[NAME OF COMPANY].

Series A Preferred Stock (the "Series A Preferred Stock").
Investors: One or more accredited investors approved by the Company (the "Investors").
Amount Raised: $[INSERT AMOUNT].
Price Per Share: $[_____] per share (based on the capitalization of the Company set forth below) (the "Original Purchase Price").
Pre-Money Valuation: The Original Purchase Price is based upon a fully diluted pre-money valuation of $[INSERT PRE-MONEY VALUATION].

(continued)

(*continued*)

Capitalization: The Company's capital structure before and after the closing of the transactions contemplated by this Term Sheet (the "Closing").

CHARTER

Dividends: Dividends will be paid on the Series A Preferred on an as-converted basis when, as, and if paid on the Common Stock.

Liquidation Preference: In the event of any liquidation, dissolution, or winding up of the Company, the proceeds shall be paid as follows:

First pay one times the Original Purchase Price plus declared and unpaid dividends on each share of Series A Preferred (or, if greater, the amount that the Series A Preferred would receive on an as-converted basis). The balance of any proceeds shall be distributed pro rata to holders of Common Stock.

A merger or consolidation (other than one in which stockholders of the Company own a majority by voting power of the outstanding shares of the surviving or acquiring corporation) and a sale, lease, transfer, exclusive license, or other disposition of all or substantially all of the assets of the Company will be treated as a liquidation event (a "**Deemed Liquidation Event**"), thereby triggering payment of the liquidation preferences described above, unless the holders of at least a majority of the Series A Preferred elect otherwise.

Voting Rights: The Series A Preferred shall vote together with the Common Stock on an as-converted basis, and not as a separate class, except (i) **so long as at least 50 percent of Series A Preferred shares are outstanding,** the Series A Preferred as a class shall be entitled to elect one member of the Board (the "**Series A Director**"), **and** (ii) as required by law. The Company's Certificate of Incorporation will provide that the number of authorized shares of Common Stock may be increased or decreased with the approval of a majority of the Preferred and Common Stock, voting together as a single class, and without a separate class vote by the Common Stock.

Protective Provisions: **So long as at least 50 percent of the** shares of Series A Preferred are outstanding, **in addition to any other vote or approval required under the Company's Charter or Bylaws,** the Company will not, without the written consent of the holders of at least a majority of the Company's Series A Preferred, either directly or by amendment, merger, consolidation, or otherwise:

(i) liquidate, dissolve, or wind up the affairs of the Company, or effect any merger or consolidation or any other Deemed Liquidation Event; (ii) amend, alter, or repeal any provision of the Certificate of Incorporation or Bylaws in a manner materially adverse to the Series A Preferred; (iii) create or authorize the creation of or issue any other security convertible into or exercisable for any equity security, having rights, preferences, or privileges senior to or on parity with the Series A Preferred, or increase the authorized number of shares of Series A Preferred; (iv) purchase or redeem or pay any dividend on any capital stock prior to the Series A Preferred, other than stock repurchased from former employees or consultants in connection with the cessation of their employment/ services, at the lower of fair market value or cost; other than as approved by the Board; or (v) create or authorize the creation of any debt security if the Company's aggregate indebtedness would exceed $[___]; (vi) **create or hold capital stock in any subsidiary that is not a wholly owned subsidiary or dispose of any subsidiary stock or all or substantially all of any subsidiary assets; or (vii)** increase or decrease the size of the Board of Directors.

(*continued*)

(*continued*)

Optional Conversion: The Series A Preferred initially converts 1:1 to Common Stock at any time at option of holder, subject to adjustments for stock dividends, splits, combinations, and similar events and as described below under "Conversion Price Adjustments."

Conversion Price Adjustments: The holders of Series A Preferred Stock shall be entitled to broad-based weighted-average, antidilution protection, subject to customary exceptions. The conversion price of the Series A Participating Preferred Stock shall also be adjusted to reflect any stock dividends, splits, combinations, and similar events.

Mandatory Conversion: Each share of Series A Preferred will automatically be converted into Common Stock at the then applicable conversion rate in the event of the closing of a firm commitment underwritten public offering with a price of three times the Original Purchase Price (subject to adjustments for stock dividends, splits, combinations, and similar events) and gross proceeds to the Company of not less than $[30,000,000] (a "**QPO**"), or (ii) upon the written consent of the holders of greater than 50 percent of the Series A Preferred.

STOCK PURCHASE AGREEMENT

Representations and Warranties: Standard representations and warranties by the Company.

Conditions to Closing: Standard conditions to Closing, which shall include, among other things, satisfactory completion of financial and legal due diligence, qualification of the shares under applicable Blue Sky laws, and the filing of a Certificate of Incorporation establishing the rights and preferences of the Series A Preferred.

Counsel and Expenses: Company counsel to draft Closing documents. The Company and the Investors will each bear their own legal and other expenses with respect to the sale of the Series A Preferred Stock.

Company Counsel: [INSERT COMPANY COUNSEL]

Investors' Rights Agreement

Registration Rights: The holders of Common Stock obtained upon the conversion of the Series A Preferred Stock shall be entitled to piggyback and demand registration rights that are customary in transactions similar in nature to those described herein.

Information Rights: Any Major Investor (who is not a competitor) will be granted access to Company facilities and personnel during normal business hours and with reasonable advance notification. The Company will deliver to such Major Investor (i) annual, quarterly, and monthly financial statements, and other information as determined by the Board; (ii) thirty days prior to the end of each fiscal year, a comprehensive operating budget forecasting the Company's revenues, expenses, and cash position on a month-to-month basis for the upcoming fiscal year; and (iii) promptly following the end of each quarter an up-to-date capitalization table. A "**Major Investor**" means any Investor who purchases at least $[INSERT AMOUNT] of Series A Preferred.

Right to Participate Pro Rata in Future Rounds: All Major Investors shall have a pro rata right, based on their percentage equity ownership in the Company (assuming the conversion of all outstanding Preferred Stock into Common Stock and the exercise of all options outstanding under the Company's stock plans), to participate in subsequent issuances of equity securities of the Company (excluding those issuances listed at the end of the "Antidilution Provisions" section of this Term Sheet). In addition, should any Major Investor choose not to

(continued)

(*continued*)

purchase its full pro rata share, the remaining Major Investors shall have the right to purchase the remaining pro rata shares.

Noncompetition and Nonsolicitation Agreements: Each Founder and key employee will enter into a one-year noncompetition and nonsolicitation agreement in a form reasonably acceptable to the Investors.

Nondisclosure and Developments Agreement: Each current and former Founder, employee, and consultant will enter into a nondisclosure and proprietary rights assignment agreement in a form reasonably acceptable to the Investors.

Board Matters: The Board of Directors shall meet at least quarterly, unless otherwise agreed by a vote of the majority of Directors.

The Company will bind D&O insurance with a carrier and in an amount satisfactory to the Board of Directors. Company to enter into Indemnification Agreement with the Series A Director and affiliated funds in form acceptable to such director. In the event the Company merges with another entity and is not the surviving corporation, or transfers all of its assets, proper provisions shall be made so that successors of the Company assume the Company's obligations with respect to indemnification of Directors.

Employee Stock Options: All new employee options to vest as follows: 25 percent after one year, with remaining vesting monthly over next 36 months.

RIGHT OF FIRST REFUSAL/COSALE AGREEMENT

Right of First Refusal/Right of Cosale (Take-Me-Along): The holders of Series A Preferred Stock shall be entitled to right of first refusal/right of cosale (take-me-along right) that are customary in transactions similar in nature to those described herein.

VOTING AGREEMENT

Board of Directors: [At the initial Closing, the Board shall consist of five members comprised of (i) [*name*] as the representative designated by the Investors, (ii) Founder/s and/or existing investor (iii) 1 individual who is not employed by the Company and who is mutually acceptable to the Founders and Investors, who shall initially be [*name*]].

Drag Along: The holders of Series A Preferred Stock shall be entitled to "drag-along" rights that are customary in transactions similar in nature to those described herein.

OTHER MATTERS

Expiration: This Term Sheet expires on [____ __], if not accepted by the Company by that date.

EXECUTED THIS [__] DAY OF [__]

[NAME OF COMPANY]

By: [NAME OF COMPANY]

By: _____

Name:

Title:

[INVESTOR]

By: _____

Name:

Title:

Terms within Term Sheets That You Need to Know

Now that we've reviewed what an actual term sheet looks like, let's look at some of the most important provisions and items in term sheets and how they differ.

Convertible Notes

Some startups will raise simple debt financing. This paperwork can essentially be standard, as with any other business, real estate, or consumer loan. More common in this space are convertible notes. This is a debt instrument that also gives the investor stock options. The flexibility of convertible notes offers security from the downside, and more potential upside if the startup performs as expected. Theoretically it can also be easier for some to justify making the loan, which has specific returns and maturity dates, versus the unknown.

Convertible notes are much faster than equity rounds. There are only two documents in place, which are the convertible note purchase agreement outlining the terms of the investment, and the promissory note explaining the conversion and the amount that the investor is investing.

With convertible notes, there are only three main ingredients that the entrepreneur needs to ensure are present.

The first ingredient is the interest that the entrepreneur is giving to the investor. This is interest to be accrued on a yearly basis on the investment amount that the investor puts into the company. The interest will continue to be applied until the company does another equity round, when the debt will convert into equity with the amount plus the interest received.

The second ingredient is the discount on the valuation. This means that if your next qualified round is at X amount of premoney valuation, the investor will be converting his or her debt at a discount from the valuation that has been established in the next round by the lead investor.

The third ingredient to watch is the valuation cap. This means that regardless of the amount that is established on the valuation in the next round, the investor will never convert north of whatever valuation cap is agreed. This is a safety measure in the event that the valuation goes through the roof. It is a good way to protect your early investors and to reward them for taking the risk of investing in you at a very early stage.

Convertible notes are, in my mind, the fastest and cheapest way to fundraise. While equity rounds can be north of $20,000, convertible notes should not cost you more than $7,000.

One thing to keep a very close eye on is the maturity date. This is the date by which you agree to repay unless you have not done a qualified round of financing in which the convertible notes are converted into equity. For this reason, make sure that the maturity date is a date that you feel confident about. You need to be convinced that you will be able to raise a qualified round of financing on or before that date in order to convert the notes into equity and avoid being in default. The last thing you want to happen is to be in default and to have to shut down your business because investors are demanding their money back.

SAFE Notes

A newer instrument that has been adopted by the likes of Y Combinator is the SAFE note. The Simple Agreement for Future Equity (SAFE) aims to increase simplicity while preserving flexibility.

Y Combinator argues that these notes do not accrue interest, or have maturity dates, which makes them friendlier to entrepreneurs. That relieves a degree of extra burden that can be counterproductive to both parties.

A SAFE note automatically converts to preferred stock at the next equity round of funding, or when there is an IPO.

Investment Tranches

Some investors obviously feel much more comfortable making their funding available in multiple payments, as opposed to handing over a $1 million check to a couple of fresh-faced cofounders with a slick pitch for a tech idea. But payment in increments can hurt cash flow, potentially making it more difficult to get through to the next milestone and round.

I have a problem with investment tranches, in particular. This is because if an investor promises to give, for example, $100,000 over the course of the next six months, and on the third month decides to pull the plug because the business is not performing well enough, there is nothing you can do. Bringing a lawsuit would slow progress and cost money (ultimately, throwing good money after bad).

Board Seats

Entrepreneurs can expect significant investors to request seats on the board of directors. The founders and investors may have ownership, but the board of directors really has control.

If you were putting a sizable amount of money into a young company, you'd like to have a say in major decisions, too. However, it's critical for entrepreneurs to think about the big picture. You can't give away too many board seats. You don't want board meetings to become a nightmare. You want to be sure the board you have isn't a turnoff to future investors. So fill the seats on your board with care.

You can also invite people to serve as board observers. This means they can attend board meetings but won't have a vote in various matters. This can become complicated, as the investor might be particularly outspoken and may influence board members who do have a vote.

Antidilution Provisions

For investors, dilution can be both a necessary part of business growth and a source of fear. *Full ratchet* and *weighted* are two common terms you'll find in this provision of the term sheet. Be cautious here, and understand how antidilution clauses may impact your own profitability and the potential for raising additional funding later.

For the most part, antidilution provisions are not reasonable to have at an early stage. In the event the company goes through different rounds of financing, it is then more common to have this provision for the founder so that he or she is still motivated to stay, in the event that the founder's equity decreases substantially.

Miscellaneous Terms and Clauses

Consent to sell, first right of refusal, and *cosale limitations* can all be part of a term sheet. While there are some open source term sheets available, each one can be different. This makes it particularly important that founders read and reread each term sheet in its entirety, and have their legal counsel review it.

Sample term sheets can be found online at www.seriesseed.com, www.techstars.com/docs, and via the National Venture Capital Association. Each of these resources offer forms that are evenly balanced for both entrepreneur and investor.

Feel free to compare the different samples with the example provided in this chapter. I strongly suggest you look at the documents with legal counsel by your side.

Term Sheet Tactics

What smart strategies should founders have when going into the term sheet stage? What investor tactics should they beware of?

Red Flag Terms to Watch Out For

When a founder is so close to ending the round and getting the precious funding that everyone has worked so hard for, it can cause some actors to rush and overlook critical terms and indicators that can potentially set the company up for disaster.

Several times in this book, we've highlighted the need to watch out for predatory investors. This is definitely one of those times. Bad terms may be thrown in simply because investors don't know better. In other cases, this may be due to ulterior motives. Specifically look out for:

- Harsh debt financing and convertible note terms that could bankrupt you
- Asking for too large a controlling stake, which may suggest you'll be replaced
- Terms that can limit further fundraising
- Investors that simply want a short and hot exit, and don't have realistic expectations of timelines

Investors may aim to exhaust a founder who's eager to wrap things up. If you see this is happening to you, hang in and be patient. Every single provision included in documents may not make sense today, but one of them may be triggered in the long run and put you, your cofounders, and other employees in a bad space.

A piece of advice: Be unattached to the outcome. You should be prepared to walk away if you see that the investor is overtly using tactics to wear you down during the process. This could show up in the form of negotiating a clause again, or introducing something new at the last minute.

Smart Term Sheet Strategies

Just as founders don't want difficult or greedy investors on board, investors don't want hassle or founders who only want to take the money and run. The term sheet should facilitate a win-win for both sides.

Negotiating and getting the best deal is smart, and good business, too. If you don't show any business sense, then how is an investor going to trust that you will be able to run a profitable organization and protect his investment? Investors deserve and expect respect.

While every investor is keen on honing in and finding that big win, there are plenty of startups looking for funding. So keep in mind, no matter how weary you may be, that being too difficult and making the terms unattractive won't help you achieve your goals.

Think about what is most important in advance. What do you want the outcome to be? Do you really want this investor on board, or are you just happy raising money from anyone, provided it is on your terms? How much does timing and speed matter? What happens if this deal falls through? What balance between upside potential, downside protection, and ease of dealing with you will optimize the transaction, and help you to ensure that you get what you want most?

For example, should you go in with a mindset that you'll give up a good amount of equity in order to land this investor? Should you pull out some of the quirky terms and cheesy tactics like short expiration dates to present yourself better? Put yourself in the investor's shoes, and ask what will get him to expedite.

The rule of thumb is that you will be receiving a dilution of around 20 percent per round of financing. You do not want to go over that amount. The life of a startup is long. Even if you are at a seed stage and you feel it is okay to give up a good amount of equity, you need to know that equity will not come back to you.

I would also recommend avoiding greed. As Mark Cuban has said, "It is much better to have 1 percent of $1 billion than 100 percent of nothing."

If Things Don't Go Forward

A term sheet itself (without signatures) is not an executed deal, or even a promise. There is still due diligence to be done. So both sides can walk away and it doesn't necessarily impact the reputation of either side.

They made an offer, you made yours, and you couldn't meet in the middle. But don't talk badly about the investor just because you didn't like the terms. The next prospective investor in line might question what you'll say about her if she sends you a term sheet. So be mindful. And once you do shake hands on a deal, remember that your word and reputation is really the most valuable thing you've got. It's the only thing you've got.

Some investors will reinvest in future ventures with the same founders—even if they lost money the first time—if they trust them and like them.

But if you don't honor your word, no one is going to bet on you.

One investing nightmare that tends to recur is when founders receive a term sheet and think the deal is done. They start increasing expenses, thinking the money will be transferred. I've personally witnessed instances where a founder with a term sheet ended up not closing the deal, and the founder had to shut down because it was assumed that the money was already in place. Do not be one of these cases.

13

Closing the Deal

ALL OF YOUR HARD WORK, preparation, and research has led you to this one pivotal point of your entrepreneurial career—closing the deal.

No matter how well you have pitched your business to investors, it is always possible for a deal to fall through, even at the last minute. This fact is not mentioned here to alarm you, but to instead keep you vigilant and to ensure that you continue to make appropriate decisions, regarding how you present your company to investors, right up until the last possible second.

The Importance of Urgency

A business deal should not be rushed into quickly without fore-thought; however, your preparations and any required due diligence should be in order by the time you have come to completing the deal.

Urgency at this stage is key for a number of reasons, which include:

- **Cold feet:** The more negotiations are drawn out, the greater the chance of investors getting cold feet; this is especially true when an agreement has been made in principle but has not yet been signed. If there is some impediment to closing the deal, such as securing patents, legal agreements with fellow founders, or other administrative matters, this can set alarm bells ringing in the minds of prospective investors. At this stage a quick conclusion is desirable. The more an investor has to think about a deal they have preliminarily agreed to, the greater the chance of the investor having cold feet and taking the offer off the table.

- **Options:** Another danger of dragging out the end of negotiations is that it gives investors time to weigh their options. While they wait for you to take care of what you need to do before a deal can be signed, an investor has the opportunity to look around at the competition or even other investment opportunities. It is entirely possible that they could see a similar start-up company that appears to be a more lucrative proposal and invest their money there, instead of in your business.

- **Expenses:** Finally, drawing out negotiations can result in higher expenses through legal fees; more important, it means your business is running on its current finances to survive. If you are at the planning stages of your company, then this might not matter, but if you already have staff, development, production, and other costs to cover, the longer your startup goes without new revenue, the more likely it is to suffer financially, perhaps fatally so.

Creating a Completion Schedule

A great way to move things along for both you and potential investors is to bring in a completion schedule of some kind. This is merely a proposition that clearly defines a closing date—when the deal is expected to be concluded. This creates a sense of purpose and can keep communication clear, showing all concerned parties when they can expect an agreement to become legally binding.

In order to create a completion schedule, you will want to have the following three factors in place:

1. **Time-specific breakdown:** This is a clearly defined set of dates that stipulate when aspects of a deal will come into effect. A solid schedule should be realistic and achievable. It should also take into account any perceived delays that you think are likely. If closing dates pass without any movement, this could make an investor reconsider his or her investment.

2. **Signature closing date:** This should be agreed upon between yourself and all other parties, including legal teams working on your and an investor's behalf. On that day you will both agree to have the relevant documents signed and delivered to all relevant parties. This is the day you need to aim for—when you legally have secured the investment you require to take your business to the next level.

3. **Financial closing date:** It is good business practice to have a date clearly agreed upon for any financial matters. This is the date by which you will receive an investor's capital, and that's usually after an investment agreement has become legally binding. With signatures and finances in place, you can now get on with the difficult yet rewarding job of building your startup and using investor capital to achieve immediate and/ or long-term goals.

Managing Expectations

As an important side note, expectations can be the death of a good business relationship. Without adequate communication between founders, managers, and investors, there can be no clear way of gauging how well a company is proceeding and whether it is on schedule or not.

Furthermore, the only thing worse than having no solid expectations is when founders and investors have conflicting ideas about what should be achieved and within what time frame. This is a sure way to cause confusion, but it can also be the root of serious disagreement that can undermine the success of a start-up venture.

The failure of rectifying issues with inaccurate expectations can usually be found during the negotiation phases, where ideas and time frames are not clearly stated in terms of what can be achieved with the capital being provided.

In order to avoid these difficulties it is essential that you:

- **State expectations:** First, you should have a set of your own expectations. What do you think is achievable within the confines of the investment round you are currently negotiating within? How does this relate to the "big picture" of your business? Most important, what do you think are reasonable goals and time frames that should be given in return for an agreed-upon amount of investment capital? Your expectations should be realistic and should also give you a little wiggle room for unforeseen hurdles that could set back any agreed-upon schedule. All of these expectations need to be clearly stated so that investors know exactly what they can then expect in return for their investment.

- **Listen to investors:** Now that you have given your expectations, it's time to listen to your prospective investors in a courteous manner. Remember, some investors may have valuable experience to impart in terms of business acumen, start-up experience, or marketplace knowledge. If this is the case, then it would be wasteful to not listen to them. Even if your investor is not experienced, they may still have specific ideas about what they should expect within a set timeframe. To avoid future disagreements, they need to clearly outline what they believe are acceptable requests in return for their investment—that is, product launch, market research, prototype development, advertising, and so forth.

- **Compromise:** Now that both sides have outlined their expectations, it's time to come to a consensus. Without such a consensus it may be possible that the entire deal could fall through. You may have to compromise on your expect-ations, but never agree to unreasonable or unrealistic demands. It is better to find an investor with achievable expectations than to accept the capital of an investor who may take action against you should they believe their capital is not being well managed. It's all about compromise, and only then can you manage expectations. In order to do this, you'll have to update your investors regularly on business developments.

Updating Your Investors

While this is technically a part of managing expectations, it's such an important aspect that it deserves to be explored in greater detail. If there is one thing you should take away from this chapter it is that communication is key.

You have to communicate with your investors throughout the negotiation period, but also after securing investment. This ensures that misunderstandings will be avoided, and is a best practice to cultivate an organized approach to time management and reaching company milestones with available investment.

Before you have concluded and signed off on an investment agreement, you will need to inform potential investors of any delays and why they have happened. This will help to create a trustworthy, open atmosphere between yourself as a startup founder, and the investor—a climate that will act as a positive foundation for future discussions and interactions.

Once a deal has been completed, the truly hard work begins. How often you update investors about developments will depend on the investor. Some will require quarterly updates, others will want to hear what's happening on a weekly, perhaps even daily basis. You will need to agree to an update schedule and stick to it.

When updating investors, you should include:

- Any issues that have presented themselves
- New organizational changes that are being made

- Answering any queries that investors have raised recently
- Press coverage
- New business development deals and partnerships
- Milestones achieved
- Milestones for the next quarter
- Growth in terms of users and revenues
- Potential new hurdles and challenges down the line
- Details of any financial changes including running costs
- Requests and asks that you would like to make from the investor

If you and an investor have decided to stay in contact regularly, then updates may be less detailed, building upon each other. On the other hand, if an investor wants an update only when something important is happening, then your report may be more in-depth, as it will have more to cover.

Closing the Deal Is Not the End of the Deal

As you can see, there is much to think about when closing a deal. Most important, this stage can act as a template for your relationship with an investor. As with many things in life, it's always best to make a good impression right away and to remember that a successful entrepreneur will be as communicative as possible.

Raising money and closing a round of financing should never be viewed as a milestone. It is more of a stepping-stone that can help to get you, your team, and your investors to the next step on the journey.

14

Avoiding Common Fundraising Mistakes

MOST OF THIS BOOK HAS BEEN FOCUSED on what to do in order to effectively raise capital. But it is equally important to learn from others' mistakes, and to take to heart the lessons that can be learned.

What are some of the common mistakes made in the fundraising process that should be avoided?

Failing to Connect

Lacking connections puts startups and their founders at a serious disadvantage. Do not underestimate the value of connections!

Business (and fundraising in particular) is still more often about whom you know, not what you know, so invest in making connections and building relationships. When I was first starting out, I would never miss an opportunity to attend an industry event and give talks or provide insights or commentary. This would ultimately increase my reach and network.

The ability to connect carries over to circulating your investment opportunity, as well as following up. Previous chapters discuss

153

some of the things to look for and to avoid in an investor. It's wise to screen for investors who have domain expertise, are well connected themselves, and have financial strength. Yet, even before pitching, startups need to make sure that they are connecting with and presenting to the right investors. Do you have an Ideal Investor Profile?

Startups should have an Ideal Investor profile for each fundraising round. Factors to consider may include:

- Location
- Average size of investments
- Industry match
- Round of funding the investor specializes in
- Investment goals and timeline

The above will all help startups, even when connecting and pitching new investor contacts, because it's part of creating a good fit. That's going to feel a lot better for you. Even if they don't invest, you should get some valuable feedback rather than simply being dismissed because your startup doesn't fit that investor's criteria.

When you are in the fundraising process, it is ultimately not only about the capital: It comes down to value. This is a good opportunity for you to cover some of the holes that you didn't realize existed in your plans. This may come from potential customers or existing customers. You will need to cut through the noise and get the best feedback and share it with your team in order to improve some aspects of the business. Moreover, it will be a good chance for you to shape up the pitch and the way you are telling your story.

This is also a building block for delivering your pitch and effective follow-up. Cold spamming investors is likely to be more counterproductive than helpful. As already mentioned, there are a few stunning success stories in which entrepreneurs have managed to get emails through to investors like Mark Cuban and get funded. But whether making initial contact or following up, it will be those who personalize their messages who will be successful. This means pitching the right opportunity to the right investor and in the right language. Cuban is one of the easiest examples because most are pretty familiar with how he speaks and his style.

Venture capital firms, for example, place a lot of weight on the introduction. They use this as social proof. Depending on who is introducing you, they will take your pitch more or less seriously. Normally you would want to have the introduction from a founder who has given an exit (which means a startup in which the firm has invested money and received a good amount in returns).

In any case, people do appreciate entrepreneurs who will make the effort to hunt them down and follow up. And sometimes this is a test of your grit and innovation skills. On the *Ignite Your Sales Team* podcast, Rich Cohen, who is a sales leader for Tony Robbins' Robbins Research, says that he'll purposely blow candidates off, and see who will be successful at getting through to him on the phone, getting into his office, or rebutting him over email. So make connections, connect in a way they can relate to, and follow up.

Clarity and Doing What You Say

We live in a crazy time, an era in which it is incredibly difficult to find anyone or any company that will do what they say or have promised. This is what has created immunity and aversion to advertising. You go into the car dealer after seeing an ad and by the time you leave, that $399/month lease on the new Tough Rider is closer to $999/month, plus about the same amount again in a deposit and insurance, instead of the "no money down" sign-and-drive deal you expected. You sign up for a new cable TV and Internet service that guarantees 24-hour response times, and then that $29-a-month deal winds up being closer to $100/month, if the product ever works or you can ever get someone to provide service. Or you switch your cell-phone service to an "all-inclusive" plan for $150 a month, and then get a $3,000 bill for roaming and extra data charges and taxes.

You know what that feels like. It doesn't matter if it comes down to a lack of clarity or straight-up being hustled, it doesn't feel good, right? It makes you not only want to tear up that contract, but sell off your shares in that company, even at a loss, just to stick it to them. And you'll be sure to share the negative experience with everyone you know.

It all comes down to some of the most basic strong emotions we have, like fear and shame. No one wants to be made a fool of. That is more of a driver than the financial side. No investor wants what they believe to be a "great investment" to become a frustrating embarrassment. To overcome this, startups and their founders must be in alignment, deliver clarity, and stay congruent. It comes down to one word and that is "integrity." Stand by your word.

Mistakes that often derail startups in this area include:

- Not having a clear pitch
- Lack of authenticity
- Lying
- Changing your story
- Overpromising
- Overselling
- Name dropping without having much of a relationship with the individuals
- Spamming

When it comes to raising venture capital, I'm commonly talking about fundraising from people and organizations with vast differences in culture, location, and perception. So you can't assume that people know what you mean, or what you are thinking. You can't (and shouldn't) try to fit it all in a pitch deck, elevator pitch, or executive summary. But that doesn't mean you can't be clear and thorough.

White lies, embellishing the truth, hiding the facts, and grossly overexaggerating are all types of lying . . . period. They will destroy your reputation, credibility, and opportunity to raise funds.

Be realistic. If you are pitching a billionaire investor, multibillion dollar venture capital fund, or even an angel with several million more in the bank than you have, you can bet they probably have some level of intelligence and experience. You are not going to fool them, or win them over with grand overly optimistic revenue and market-share projections, or by hiding costs.

Many try to add a little glamor to their executive summaries or decks, and in the process they sabotage themselves. Either you are going to be seen as a fraud, or simply unrealistic and unequipped. Either way you are going to be seen as a time waster.

I like what Warren Buffett says in this regard—that it takes a lifetime to build a reputation but only five minutes to destroy it.

Have conservative profits and revenues, and maybe even higher-than-expected costs. Then you can always explain that this is your worst-case scenario or minimum expectation, but that you hope for far better results. That can win you a lot of extra points. Most VCs and investors who are experienced in your domain will easily be able to pinpoint areas where you can bulk up the right numbers, especially when they add their insights and capital.

I always recommend overdelivering. Remember that you will meet the VC and then you will follow up with them in three months or so to meet and discuss progress. At this point it would be very powerful to show how you have crushed your goals and you will get them excited. Much better than having to explain the reason behind not fulfilling what you said you would on your first meeting.

Don't change your story. You shouldn't need to if you have your entire team on board with your messaging, and you've done your own research well before putting together a plan in the first place. You might have some pivots as you go along, but multiple pivots and story changes during the middle of raising a round of funding won't make things easier.

Entrepreneurs also need to differentiate between what a real pivot or evolution of their startup plan is, and when it is just a Band-Aid covering a failed startup. Your potential investors will know.

Self-Sabotage in the Deal-Making Process

One of the biggest mistakes startups make is taking too long to complete a round. Many might find that the statistics show it can be a lot quicker to raise money than expected. Don't cut yourself short and run out of money, but don't take too long shopping around or sealing the deal with interested investors. The risk is that your deal can go stale. That money could go to someone else instead, maybe even someone else operating in your space.

Investors are like sheep. They go where everyone else is going— they see it as validation from the market. For that reason you need to build momentum and get everyone with whom you are speaking excited about your vision and where you are taking things, as soon as possible.

How long should it take to raise money? According to data from a survey published on TechCrunch, the average time to raise a seed series as of mid-2015 was 12.5 weeks. That included contacting an average of 58 investors and going to 40 investor meetings, for an average raise of $1.3 million. Yet, 17 percent of startups reported it took them over 16 weeks to get funded, with the longest time being 40 weeks.[1]

During Series A rounds, TechCrunch reported an average time-line of 9.6 weeks, with fewer meetings needed to raise the same amount of capital. One *Forbes* report recommends that entrepreneurs expect four to eight weeks to get to a "yes," for additional rounds of funding.[2]

It is interesting to see how many startups drop out of the fundraising race within a couple months, and to see those who were successful reporting taking longer than expected to raise money. A big part of being successful is sticking with it. But it is also about knowing when to hold on and when to move on.

---

[1] http://techcrunch.com/2015/06/08/lessons-from-a-study-of-perfect-pitch-decks-vcs-spend-an-average-of-3-minutes-44-seconds-on-them/#.wcqqmt:VmDY.

[2] www.forbes.com/sites/bryanstolle/2014/11/13/how-much-money-should-i-raise-for-my-start-up/.

Check out some crowdfunding campaigns and see how their timelines relate to their fundraising success. Glancing at some donation crowdfunding campaigns (because they are easy to compare in volume), there are some clear trends. One of these is that people can be hesitant to fund a campaign that doesn't offer a return for a full year or two . . . and this applies even if people are hoping for only a T-shirt. Momentum is a big deal. It can create that sense of urgency that gets investors to actually take action. So don't start too early or take too long.

What is really shocking is how many startups sabotage their investments after receiving offers. It can be a lot of work to get to a "yes." Even if the yes comes easy, odds are you are not going to get a second chance if you blow it. Even if you go to other investors for later rounds, they will have likely heard of you already. One of the main ways that startup founders sabotage themselves is by changing the terms. You should know what terms you can and can't work with in advance. Know your negotiating boundaries before walking into the room. Don't get greedy and try to squeeze out more after you've made an agreement.

Another turnoff is when a founder goes to the market with terms that are a little bit higher than usual. What anyone would do when this happens is decrease the price of the valuation. However, this would send negative signals to the market, where investors could interpret this as proving that you do not know what you are doing or that investors do not like your deal. Try to keep terms as attractive as possible for you and for investors.

Then there is reviewing the actual paperwork. Make no mistake—investors are in this to make money. They are in it to minimize risk and maximize upside potential. And they normally have very good lawyers to help them with the paperwork.

Founders must ensure they review each clause in the offering documents. Read all of the fine print. If you don't, you could be sabotaging your own plans. If you don't understand something, ask, get some feedback from your legal team, and don't sign until you are comfortable with an agreement.

Clearly this chapter does not provide an exhaustive list of every possible blunder, but these are some of the most important possibilities. It also highlights how important it is to ask others about their failures and mistakes, as well as their successes.

15

Understanding the JOBS Act

A lot has changed in 80 years, and it's time our laws did as well.
—Barack Obama

The signing of the Jumpstart Our Business Startups (JOBS) Act may well go down in history as one of the greatest moments during Obama's two terms in the White House. Perhaps the only ones to disagree with this are some big banks, lenders, investment salespersons, and financiers who have lost their power to the democratization of investment and fundraising.

The Game Changer

The JOBS Act, which was initially signed into law in April 2012, changed 80 years of securities regulations and legal precedents.[1]

Many forget that our financial system and organization isn't all that old. The New York Stock Exchange has been around for only 200 years. Its smaller predecessor, the London Stock Exchange, has

---

[1] https://en.wikipedia.org/wiki/Jumpstart_Our_Business_startups_Act.

161

been around for only about 300 years. Prior to that there was little organization. "Traders" met and exchanged notes in coffee houses or pooled venture capital to fund exploration and merchant ships.

The U.S. Securities and Exchange Commission (SEC) was officially founded in June 1934[2] and now regulates the industry, enforces federal security law, and poses new rules. The SEC was born out of a need to protect consumers and maintain organization, and its first chairman, Joseph Kennedy, was appointed by President Roosevelt.

While the SEC, along with the FTC (Federal Trade Commission), has certainly been a powerhouse for cracking down on bad actors and business practices, both businesses and individuals have suffered due to restrictions.

In the wake of the financial crises of the early 2000s, it was clear that businesses and the public needed more flexibility, more options, and more incentives for job creation and growth. So the JOBS Act was born with the aim of facilitating access to capital for startups and small businesses, while giving individuals more freedom to control and participate in investment opportunities, and to ultimately add more jobs to the economy.

In tearing down the barriers to fundraising and investing that hampered entrepreneurs, businesses, and investors for decades, we've ushered in a new era of democratization of finance and investing.

The JOBS Act

The Jumpstart Our Business Startups Act was specifically voted in "To increase American job creation and economic growth by improving access to the public capital markets for emerging growth companies."[3]

---

[2] https://en.wikipedia.org/wiki/U.S._Securities_and_Exchange_Commission.
[3] https://www.gpo.gov/fdsys/pkg/BILLS-112hr3606eas/pdf/BILLS-112hr3606eas.pdf.

There are seven titles to the JOBS Act:[4]

Title I: Reopening American Capital Markets to Emerging Growth Companies

Title II: Access to Capital for Job Creators

Title III: Crowdfunding

Title IV: Small Company Capital Formation

Title V: Private Company Flexibility and Growth

Title VI: Capital Expansion

Title VII: Outreach on Changes to the Law

What you need to know . . .

Title I

Title I focuses on streamlining paperwork and filing requirements for emerging growth companies (those with less than $1 billion in annual gross revenues). It also enables these companies to test the waters and promote and measure interest before incurring additional expenses.

Title II

Title II is all about general solicitation. This means that startups and other private companies are now able to publicize that they are fundraising, instead of relying solely on word of mouth within their own personal networks of accredited investors with whom they have an existing relationship.

Thanks to the implementation of Title II, which went into effect in September 2013, the flow of information can now be equally shared and consumed by the general public. The use of social media as a

---

[4] www.gpo.gov/fdsys/pkg/BILLS-112hr3606enr/pdf/BILLS-112hr3606enr.pdf.

marketing mechanism is for the first time allowed, increasing the level of translucence as the company's documentation is available on a larger scale, permitting individuals to engage in their own due diligence.

Increasing crowd involvement provides a further data point indicative of traction and interest from the public, which highly interested investors may take into consideration when deciding to move forward with an investment.

With Title II, startups with a large customer base benefit from the ability to tap into that customer base for capital support under existing regulations. These people are the biggest fans and evangelists of the brand, who might be first in line to invest. Once the user base is able to engage with their beloved company in fundraising mode via their networks or via an investment crowdfunding platform, the company is able to capitalize on the crowd's interest in their success and accelerate the fundraising process by converting customers into investors.

Publicly advertising an investment round includes, but is not limited to, the following activities:

1. Revealing that the private company is actively seeking investments
2. Providing the details of the investment, such as the deal terms
3. Revealing any additional information that is considered material for investors to know about the company in order to formulate an informed opinion.

This includes traditional and online media, such as, but not limited to:

1. A mass newsletter/email
2. A public profile on a startup investment platform
3. A company, personal, or third-party website that displays openly that a startup is fundraising
4. Public speaking engagements, such as conferences, panels, or forums

5. Social media such as Facebook, Twitter, LinkedIn, or others
6. Public videos

If startups choose to generally solicit their fundraising efforts, here are three things that they must do starting today in order to comply with the new regulations of Title II as they stand:

1. Allow only accredited investors into the funding round.

The regulations state that if you choose a Regulation D Rule 506 (b) offering, which is *private* fundraising, you can have up to 35 nonaccredited investors participating in your round, as long as you have a preexisting relationship with them. In the event you decide to carry out *public* fundraising, you relinquish that option. Only verified accredited investors are permitted to invest in startups that are generally soliciting.

2. Verify that all these investors are accredited.

This means that from the time you start general solicitation until the time you close your funding round, you will be required to provide official documentation to confirm that each investor meets the accredited investor threshold, according to the SEC requirements specified in Rule 501 of Regulation D. This can be uncomfortable and burdensome for both investors and startups, but there are third-party services that do this.

3. Declare that a 506(c) publicly advertised offering was undertaken as part of the Form D filing.

You will have to file a Form D within 15 days of receiving your first investment. This means you will have to declare that you publicly advertised your offering under new 506(c) regulations. No additional changes to this process are taking effect at this time. This could change when amendments to the proposed general solicitation rules are released, but for the moment there are no further steps to be taken for SEC filings.

In addition to the final rules that are actionable now, there are independently proposed rules that further define the requirements and procedures involved in general solicitation. On September 3, 2013, we submitted comments to the SEC, which you can read on the SEC's website, to help shape the spirit of the proposed regulations' such that it works more seamlessly with the natural flow of startups' fundraising.

Forbes coverage highlights Title II of the JOBS Act as the part that really allowed startups to begin public advertising for fundraising (aka equity crowdfunding). In the first year this saw over $250 million raised.[5]

However, criticism of these earlier enactments centered on the limitation that startups that could raise funds only from wealthier "accredited investors." Accredited investors make up only 1 percent of the U.S. population and are highly in demand as a result.[6]

The verification of accredited investor status may have also been a concern and turnoff for some startups and investors, as a startup needs to take reasonable additional measures to verify the accredited status of the investor.

Title III

Title III of the JOBS Act or the "Crowdfunding Act" focuses on Capital Raising Online While Deterring Fraud and Unethical Nondisclosure.

Title III is the real game changer, on the largest and broadest scale. Title III provides exemptions for startups and investors, enabling businesses to raise funds from nonaccredited investors. The amounts that can be raised are smaller, but dramatically increase the pool of prospective investors (99 percent of the population). This could unlock and provide startups with access to as much as 10 times current annual VC investment.

The asset class of early-stage startup equity made available on equity crowdfunding platforms is in its infancy and, soon enough,

---

[5] www.forbes.com/sites/chancebarnett/2015/03/26/infographic-sec-democratizes-equity-crowdfunding-with-jobs-act-title-iv/.

[6] http://blog.onevest.com/blog/2015/3/19/jobs-act-title-iii-and-crowdfunding-what-we-know-so-far.

will begin to look a lot like the public market's intricately woven basket of ETFs and mutual funds.

Chris Dixon, a well-respected entrepreneur who founded Hunch, which was acquired by eBay, and a partner at Andreessen Horowitz says "When you look at the biggest crowdfunding markets—publicly traded stocks on NYSE, NASDAQ, and so on—you find that in general, nonprofessional investors lose money when they try to pick individual stocks. This suggests that something similar to mutual funds would be the best mechanism for amateur participation."

To better hedge risk and maximize chances of a return on investment, dedicated funds exist today based on a particular early-stage startup industry or theme—for instance, Mobile Healthcare Fund or the Harvard Alumni Startup Fund—but it's currently restricted to high-net-worth individuals or people who qualify as accredited investors.

However, with the implementation of Title III of the JOBS Act, the general public will soon be granted access to this financial product, which offers high risk and high reward potentials, and where a lower minimum investment will make it much more accessible to Main Street. Think about it this way: For the past 80 years only accredited investors, representing 1 percent of the U.S. population (or 8 million people), were able to have access to this asset class of startup investments. With Title III implemented, over 300 million Americans will be able to invest in startups.

With an increased volume of shares purchased and traded, options markets will likely pop up—initially between larger brokers to mitigate risk, and later, individual investors will participate. As more capital begins to flood into this alternative asset class, the angel investor will be empowered by a large variety of investment products.

A typical funding round is often filled by a short list of angels and/or venture funds, who often know each other, so the pricing is heavily dependent on a handful of players, which means it has the ability to change drastically based on the mood and expectations. In contrast, by increasing the volume of shareholders and thereby exposure to a larger market, the pricing is more responsive to a deeper pool of supply and demand and has a better chance to stabilize its fair market value.

In the current state of startup investing, the sellers of equity are largely the startups themselves; but with an increased pool of shareholders, investors may be willing to divest at an early stage, post–initial investment. The ability to buy and sell these shares on the second market will increase liquidity in this sector and asset class, and thereby reduce the risk of holding what were previously highly illiquid positions.

Analysts expect equity crowdfunding to reach several trillion dollars in investment, with the potential to fund as many as 5 million startups. Note that these exemptions are limited to using an inter-mediary broker or crowdfunding portal to raise funds.

Title III also lays out rules for Funding Portals: their registration with the SEC, required memberships (FINRA), and prohibited activities, all designed to ensure safety for investors.

However, there are several concerns that I have as the regulatory landscape is drafted today. Equity crowdfunding rules limit startups to raise up to $1 million within a period of 12 months, which is a relatively short span of time given the amount of work that founders will need to do before and after the raise to comply with all the regulations.

According to CB *Insights*, seed rounds—typically a startup's first outside round of capital—are steadily increasing: "Notably, average and median seed deal sizes were on the upswing in 2014 and hit their highest levels in four years of $1.9M and $1.7M, respectively, in Q4 2014." Therefore, if the average seed deal is roughly half of the equity crowdfunding cap, founders will need to conduct additional offerings in parallel or in sequence to fulfill their funding needs, which results in additional legal costs and times.

Before even knowing if the startup will be able to successfully raise capital through equity crowdfunding, they will need to go through a series of steps to satisfy the Securities and Exchange

Commission regulations, as detailed in the final rules of equity crowdfunding.

In assessing the burden the businesses will have to undergo in order to be able to rely on the new equity crowdfunding rules, the Commission estimates that on average 100 work hours will be required to prepare the proper filings (a combination of work done both internally and by professionals). The cost associated with this preparation range between $6,000 and $20,000.

Additionally, as part of the preround filing requirements, depending on how many funds are targeted for the raise, various financial statements will be required. Any business raising more than $500,000, which is likely the majority given the typical seed round size trending upwards of nearly $2 million, will require audited financials, which can cost between $10,000 and $40,000.

Then there are periodic raise updates that are required to be filed: while some can be done through intermediaries, others cannot. The most pressing update is the annual report requirement. It's estimated to take between 50 and 95 hours of work each year for the remaining time of a company's existence (unless there is an event that would cause the reporting requirement to cease, at which point another filing must be done), and its costs can range anywhere between $7,000 and $25,000 per year.

A detailed due diligence screening conducted by the intermediaries or their outsourced partners will need to take place, which can take anywhere between 15 and 90 days. It will examine every little aspect of the company, its officers, and its major stakeholders, which, depending on whether the intermediary does this in-house or outsources it, will result in additional fees typically ranging between $2,000 to $5,000.

To build on top of that, there is no good way of making this process truly scalable as an operator as each due diligence conducted is unique to the company undergoing it. There is a lot of time and work required on the founder's side, which can slow their fundraising efforts. This is especially true since, for the most part, funding portals operating for accredited investors currently do not take the whole round, as they act as fillers of an already existing round of financing.

A company's capitalization table specifically outlines the entire equity and debt ownership of a business, as well as liquidation rankings of investors and/or lenders. Keeping a clean capitalization table (cap table) is key. The fewer investors you have to herd to get major decisions approved and things signed, the better. The most common practices utilized to help keep cap tables clean are to monitor the minimum investment from each investor and group smaller investors into a special purpose vehicle (SPV) that in turn invests in the startup directly. Via the SPVs a company can group as much as 99 investors into a single entity where one single managing member is in charge of the signature in representation of the other individuals that are part of the SPV.

As an alternative to SPVs, there are ways to limit the voting rights and so forth of a particular offering, but it's not ideal for the investors and it clutters the cap table. For companies looking to do subsequent rounds of financing, it may be challenging to add on top-tier institutional investors due to fears about the additional paperwork, compliance with regulations, and increased liability that comes with having nonaccredited investors participating.

Given the serious time commitment, cost, and risk in raising capital through Title III of the Jobs Act, founders will inevitably weigh their options in accessing capital. The traditional funding route via accredited angel investors is relatively straightforward, costing from $5,000 to $20,000 with approximately a few weeks of preparation time required to get the financials, pitch deck, and offering documents ready. In comparison, when you add up the preparation work required ahead of the fundraising and the ongoing reporting requirements, depending on the amount being raised, the costs could be anywhere between $20,000 and $250,000 or more, not counting the internal man hours required to comply with the regulations.

Among many other things, intermediaries that decide to move into the nonaccredited investor market will assume a higher level of liability than there was in dealing only with accredited investors.

Whether it's right or wrong, in the eyes of the law accredited investors are considered *sophisticated* people and they bear some of the risk of venturing into unregulated investments, such as venture investing.

Unlike donation crowdfunding, in which there are no securities sold, equity crowdfunding is tremendously regulated. Everything is done under a microscope, and there are very strict rules around how intermediaries can be compensated as well as how you are allowed to incentivize others to help grow the distribution channels.

While the intentions of Title III of the Jobs Act were beneficial and grandiose in nature, the direct involvement of financial regulators is creating too many obstacles that need to be overcome both by startups and intermediaries to make this a fruitful avenue to raise capital.

According to the Commission's estimate, only 1,900 businesses will raise capital via equity crowdfunding per year. When you stack that up against the total number of deals that were funded in 2014, which is 73,400, this means that less than 2 percent of startups will go through the hurdles to raise capital from nonaccredited investors.

Title IV

The provisions under this portion of the JOBS Act cover disclosures, issuance of equity, debt, and convertible securities, and most notably Regulation A+.

Under Title IV, Regulation A+ is a newly revamped securities regulation that companies can rely on to raise up to $50 million from accredited and nonaccredited investors alike. In traditional funding (Regulation D, Rule 506 (b)/(c) offerings), companies are either limited to having up to 35 nonaccredited investors in their round or be completely banned from onboarding nonaccredited investors altogether. Accredited investors make up less than 1 percent of the U.S. population, meaning 99 percent of people previously couldn't invest in startups even if they understood the risk and had the liquid capital to deploy.

Regulation A has been around for years, but has not been widely used mainly because of the way the rules were written, making raising capital quite inefficient. In fact, the Securities and Exchange Commission (SEC) estimated only 26 offerings were conducted annually and they were capped at an upper funding limit of $5 million. Whereas now, with Regulation A+, companies can raise up to $20 million on Tier 1 and up to $50 million on Tier 2, which changes the game.

If you go with a Regulation A+ offering, everyone will be able to invest in the business, from your hairdresser or dentist to traditional angel investors and institutions. So this new fundraising outlet is truly complementary to how the typical fundraising process unfolds.

If you have a customer or user base that loves your brand, inviting them to invest allows them to have an ownership stake in your company, so you get two for the price of one. It deepens the loyalty of your customers and gives them a reason to be even bigger evangelists for the success of your business. You are onboarding investors who really believe in what you are creating, as opposed to only wanting a return on their investment: It's like investing with a cause.

Raising money under Regulation A+ can be complicated. Rightfully so, the SEC has many rules around how private securities are sold to the general public, in order to protect people from fraudulent offerings. As restrictions around who can invest are relaxed, the level of required documentation that is to be made available has also increased. Here are some of the more critical things you should know about what is required to raise under Regulation A+:

- Location: Your company must be incorporated within the United States.
- Cost: It could cost between $50,000 to $100,000 just to get everything ready for fundraising. Required documentation includes: offering documents, offering circular, GAAP/audited financials, due diligence performed, various filings with the SEC, and more, depending on your specific situation.

- Stage: Your company should be past the point where it is raising seed funds to build your product/business. You should now be looking to raise or already be raising a Series A or later stage offering.
- Financials: Your company must work with expert independent accountants to prepare audited financial statements (under Tier 2), organize your cap table, and provide a clean auditor's report.

In my opinion, Regulation A+ is appealing for companies to essentially do a public offering without having to pony up the capital and legal muscle to file the S-1 to do an Initial Public Offering (IPO), which can run in the millions of dollars, not to mention take several months. Although there is good information online explaining the requirements for raising under Tier I or Tier 2 offerings, if you are considering raising capital using Regulation A+, it is critical that you partner with seasoned funding platforms or registered broker dealers who have the know-how to conduct the raise in a fully compliant manner. Selling securities to the public must be done with caution and in line with securities regulations.

Implications for Startups and Raising Money Online

As with everything else in the financial, investment, fundraising, and startup ecosystem in which we live and operate, the JOBS Act, its titles, and implementation, is constantly evolving.

However, there is no question that this act is a major game changer for startup fundraising, and the economy in general.

When evaluating the different sources of capital, the JOBS Act definitely tips the scales in favor of crowdfunding, at least for a significant part of a startup's fundraising plans.

To sum up the JOBS Act and its implications for startups and entrepreneurs, it primarily means streamlining the process and improving the cost effectiveness of growth and raising capital, all at great scale. Whether you are brainstorming a brand-new venture or already have a mid-sized business approaching $1 billion in revenues, the JOBS Act could allow for one of the most efficient methods of gaining extra funds—via online crowdfunding.

Even aside from the Internet aspect, the JOBS Act enables private companies to now publicly solicit investors—not only accredited investors, along with the burden that carries, but from among the wider public, too. That is essentially a 9,900 percent increase in the number of prospective investors for your startup. In theory this also dramatically increases the chances of success in fundraising. In reality, there will still be some need to target and home in to connect with the right investors for most startups, at least for the sake of time and efficiency.

Even the brief overview of the JOBS Act provided here should make it clear that navigating all of the provisions and fine print alone can be a complex task. Via *Realty411 Magazine*, securities attorney veteran Gene Trowbridge reminds us that there are several options and rule allowances to launch under, and that it is both essential to find the right fit in terms of regulations and also to be aware that the JOBS Act isn't a green light to rush out and start offering investment opportunities to the general public. The chances are that you will still be filing with the SEC first, or using a registered Funding Portal that is registered with the SEC.

It really doesn't have to be that complicated if you have a good guide, but it is critical to begin on the right foot, and make sure you are on the right side of the law and regulators.

Finally, look for a crowdfunding portal that checks all the boxes required by the SEC and JOBS Act, which has a proven track record of success and can provide all the details of how they cover you and ensure compliance for your fundraising efforts.

Additional answers to frequently asked questions can be found at www.SEC.gov.

Implications for Individual Investors

The side effect of the JOBS Act and democratization of fundraising and investing may be putting a dent in the power of VCs, banks, financial brokers, and their pocketbooks. But this is certainly a giant win for both sophisticated and experienced investors, as well as the average individual. This is not simply a pivot or tweak to features: It alters the DNA of the economy.

Via crowdfunding portals, individual investors can now take full control over their investments and retirement savings. It isn't just a matter of choice, either. The cost savings and efficiencies realized by businesses can be passed on and realized by individuals, which means that they can invest faster, in what they choose, with more transparency, and for more value and better returns.

This appeal, value, and snowballing trend can't be ignored by companies. It must be factored in as founders compare fundraising options. Now investors are as much customers as are those who buy products or services, so recognize what they are looking for and where they are spending their time and funds.

In my opinion, what is really exciting for investors is the fact that you do not need to be a Silicon Valley insider in order to access great deal flow. You can now do it online. Moreover, you do not need to invest the typical amount that would be required in the offline world (which ranges between $50,000 and $150,000). Now you can allocate all that amount in different startups, and diversify, which reduces the amount of risk and lets you hedge your bets.

16

Recommended Tools for Fundraising

THERE HAS NEVER BEEN A better time in history to be an entrepreneur. The Internet provides countless helpful tools and websites that can inform, and even guide, a startup businessperson on his or her journey toward business goals, especially when looking to raise investment capital.

Even more amazing are the countless opportunities for success without a huge amount of capital. Take, for example, the costs of servers back in the day. You needed at least a few million to keep a decent-size Internet business in full force. Now for $5,000 you can have those costs covered.

Using the Right Tools

There are some fantastic websites and services out there that will help you better organize your business and structure the entire process of attracting and finalizing investment.

With this in mind, you will find a list of programs and websites to assist you below, categorized into relevant sections to make finding what you need easier. When you are in fundraising mode you ultimately want to reduce the amount of time to close investors, and be as effective and productive as possible with every single minute you are investing in the process.

Organization

We'll tackle organizational tools and websites first, as these will help you develop a structured work ethic and infrastructure. With this in place, all of your decision making will be faster, more streamlined, and more effective. Useful resources to help with organization include:

- **Google apps:** Google provides a range of applications for budding and established entrepreneurs, many of which are available for free or at low cost. What's more, all of these applications integrate with each other to increase productivity and communication across your company. Gmail is an excellent email service, while Google Hangouts allows you to video chat with investors, colleagues, and vendors from around the world without leaving your office. Google Apps also provides users with a powerful suite of office tools that will allow you to create, edit, and share documents and presentations within your team.
- **Cloud storage:** This type of storage is incredibly important. Cloud storage allows you to backup your documents and files from anywhere, uploading them onto a secure online server. This allows you to work collectively on projects with your team, while maintaining a safe backup of important files that you can access wherever there is an Internet connection or mobile service. A number of cloud storage services are available, with the two most popular being Dropbox and Google Drive (which is a part of Google Apps).
- **Open office:** This free office suite is a great alternative to Microsoft Office for those on a budget. It provides a first-class

word processor to create documents; a spreadsheet editor, which is an indispensable tool for keeping track of investors, investment amounts, and your startup's budget, as well as carrying out accounting tasks; a tool for creating PowerPoint presentations that can be used as part of your pitch to wow potential investors; a program to design and draw promotional materials and logos; as well as a database creator and editor, which is great for keeping track of large amounts of information about your business and investment pitches.

- **Remote desktop:** There are a number of great remote access programs available. These will allow you to access your PC remotely from any device. As a startup entrepreneur you may want to show a colleague how to complete a task on their computer, or access data centers from across the globe, or perhaps you are on the go and need the power of your desktop PC in your smartphone. TeamViewer, Remote Utilities, and AeroAdmin all offer great software to help you with just that.
- **Task management:** Whether you are developing your pitch, attempting to reach milestones during a micro seed investment phase, or simply trying to stay on top of the day-to-day running of your business, task management software can be a big help. With a task manager you can set larger goals for your project and systematically progress through smaller milestones, using them as a map on your way to success. Services such as Trello, Producteev, and Asana will allow you to keep your startup on track, as well as ensure that you are moving in the right direction during each investment round, and keeping a detailed record of what your startup has accomplished so far, and what it needs to accomplish in the future.

I remember when we raised our own round of funding on our own platform and what I had to do in order to streamline the process completely and automate whatever I could.

I went ahead and created different lists with existing contacts and with other people whom I wanted to target.

- One list was done via the creation of a Google Script that would crawl through all the emails that I had sent from my Gmail account.
- There was another list with VCs and other people that I have been emailing over time, including existing investors.
- The other list was made up of investors that were accredited from our user base, where I had a preexisting relationship.

Once the targeted leads were emailed, the next part of the process was to create templates or canned responses to respond quickly to all the emails that I was receiving. (You can use applications such as Boomerang or TouttApp for this.) Otherwise it would have been impossible to deal with the volume of people who were replying back to me with either more questions or comments that required replies in order to get the investor to the next step of the funnel.

Always remember that fundraising is sales. I look at sales as a funnel that includes different steps within phases investors go through. You need to keep track of those steps and address investors according to the phase they are in.

Besides the "no" responses and the questions that I would receive, which were usually the same, I would use ScheduleOnce to schedule meetings on the phone and to avoid the back-and-forth in coordinating a time. Some of the meetings were on the phone, others at the office or at remote locations. The time of the meetings would range from 15 minutes to 45 minutes.

After the initial phone call, people would then:

- Request access to the deal room, if they did not have access already
- Say they needed some time to think about the potential deal
- Say they were not interested and disregard further communication
- Request the offering documents for execution

I would then go on to create a pipeline where I would organize leads in the following manner:

- People who have wired the funds
- People who have signed the offering documents but not wired the funds
- People who have requested access to the deal room
- People who were interested

Once you have everyone listed in different categories, then you know how to treat them, and ultimately, it is a matter of putting leads into what I call the Follow-up Game. This means sending a follow-up email on a weekly or biweekly basis, sharing some exciting news and progress of the business or financing round.

The last part of the process is to complete the closing of the entire round and wrap up the administrative side, which is burdensome.

Research

In planning your pitch, it is desirable to have market research and financial figures to showcase the potential customer base for your brand, as we covered in earlier chapters. There are various services available that will help you put these important projections in place. Some of these include:

- **Manta:** A free website that is a great resource for business advice. More specifically, if your startup is going to sell from business to business, Manta has information regarding 24 million businesses in the United States alone. It can help you research the market you will be trading in as you make use of revenue, employee numbers, geography, and other important business statistics about your competitors or potential vendors/customers.

- **Google Analytics:** If your website is already up and running, Google Analytics will provide you with insightful data about your visitors. This will help in defining the most responsive demographics for your brand, which can then be used during negotiations to clearly define the target demographics you believe your product or service will have most leverage with. It will also help you decipher which types of promotional content are engaging with those demographics the most.
- **Bplans:** This is a fantastic resource which will help you to create an effective business plan, while offering free industry reports to help you devise a more streamlined pitch, showing investors why your industry is fertile ground for new investment.

Social Media

We've mentioned this in previous chapters, but social media is a great way to generate buzz about your startup and to identify prospective investors. It provides the perfect opportunity to engage effectively with people, building your brand and presenting your business in an appealing way for customers and investors alike. Useful social media platforms for fundraising include:

- **LinkedIn:** This professional network is a fantastic way to identify potential investors and to grow your network of industry-relevant contacts. It is designed for entrepreneurs and business-minded individuals to present their skills and experience in a way that can attract employers and/or investors. With a few strategic searches, you should be able to compile a list of potential investors and follow leads with securing investment capital in mind.
- **Twitter:** As a social media platform, Twitter is one of the most popular avenues for businesses to engage with customers, but it can be a great tool for startup entrepreneurs to contact potential investors as well. By retweeting and entering into conversations with those who are connected to your chosen

industry, you can quickly build a network and increase the visibility of your company. The more visible it is, the more chance it will have of attracting investors, especially if your brand has an established following.

- **Facebook:** As the most popular social media platform in the world, Facebook is an extremely important website for businesses, with unique opportunities for networking and engaging with customers. First of all, through Facebook business pages, your startup can establish a well-presented online presence quickly, with a minimum of resources. This can then be used as part of your pitch, especially if you have already amassed a number of followers, showing that there will be interest in your product/service when launched. Second, it's a great way to network with professionals, companies, and investors, sounding them out for cross-promotional ties and potential investment.

Outsourcing

One of the greatest lessons a startup entrepreneur can learn is when to delegate responsibilities. When it's your business, it can be hard to let go of every detail, but it is best to employ people to carry out tasks they are specialized in, rather than spreading yourself too thin.

By bringing talented individuals into your startup on a task-by-task basis, you will increase productivity and free up time to focus on the big picture and direction of your business. You could hire a seasoned finance writer to help create a business plan or a graphic designer to create a logo for your startup, not to mention the thousands of skilled workers who could take care of any number of important administrative duties; and as they are working as freelancers, you engage their services only when you need to. There are some great outsourcing services available such as:

- **Upwork:** As a reminder, Upwork allows a business owner to post job advertisements for tasks they need carried out, or to headhunt talented individuals with proven track records. Rates of pay vary widely, but for the most part they are very reasonable, and with Upwork's excellent Teamroom app, you can ensure that you are only billed for work as it's being done.

■ **99 Designs:** While Upwork is a good all-rounder, 99 Designs specializes in putting business owners in touch with graphic designers. This is a great medium for finding designers who will create a unique, quality presentation of your business through logos, illustrations, concept designs, and other materials perfect for promotion and fundraising. This is an excellent option if you are not prototype ready, and require a visual representation of a product to show prospective investors.

Sales and Administration

Finally, there are some great resources to help with selling your business to investors and customers, as well as carrying out the essential legally binding administrative tasks that every startup founder should take seriously. Such services include:

■ **Toutapp:** Whether you are selling to a customer or trying to attract investment, the objective is the same—to persuade an individual that you possess something worthwhile. Toutapp is a great service that allows you to track your sales, close deals faster through a suite of productivity tools, and analyze your sales process so that you can increase the efficacy of your investment pitch. The beauty of Toutapp is that it will help to streamline your business throughout each investment round and beyond.

■ **HelloSign:** Many of your customer, employee, and investor interactions will take place remotely. You could be speaking with prospective investors on the other side of the globe, yet you need a quick, secure, and legally binding way to commit a signature to appropriate documentation. This is exactly what

HelloSign does, removing the need for paper documents and slower, more laborious administrative processes.

Finding Your Investors

The tools we have mentioned so far are great ways to help you organize and interact with your customers and investors. Now what you really need is an effective way to find prospective investors.

One tried and tested approach is to use a crowdsourcing model. Crowdsourcing websites attract investors and startup businesses from around the world. They work by:

- Providing a virtual marketplace for investors to peruse start-ups across a variety of budgets and sectors.
- Giving startup founders a place to showcase their businesses in a way that makes them more enticing to investors.
- Matching investors and founders based on common business interests, deadlines, and finances.
- Nurturing communication by giving founders and investors a positive, effective, and easy-to-use forum to discuss a project.
- Helping founders and investors throughout the negotiation phase by offering advice and consultation with the aim of ensuring all parties are satisfied, before investment is secured.

There are a few different crowdsourcing sites available, and they really do take the stress out of trying to find an investor, while assisting founders with their experience with the startup market.

17

Red Flags

FOR THOSE READY TO POWER forward, recognizing red flags is as important as knowing what to do when it comes to raising capital quickly and effectively.

Key Red Flags for Startups

In our coverage of what to look for in investors we touched on some of these red flags:

- Time wasters
- Lack of experience
- Asking for far too much
- Offering too little
- Too pushy

As you now know, look for investors that are going to be an asset beyond the money. Some may claim that you don't have to like your investors, just their finances. But a lack of mutual interest will likely lead to problems.

Red Flags for Investors

In order to ensure a successful and streamlined fundraising, experienced entrepreneurs also need to be alert to what investors may perceive as red flags.

Too Many Members of the Founding Team

Giving equity is a great way to motivate and enroll the help of more individuals when your startup is lean on cash. This can be applied to cofounders, key team members, friends and family investors in the seed stage, and even advisors and professionals such as lawyers. However, too much equity in the hands of too many (especially inexperienced) early shareholders can be problematic. Even too many team members at the beginning can be problematic from an investor's point of view. So keep your fundraising goals in mind when hiring and considering bringing on cofounders.

Overhead Is Too High

If overhead is already too high, or the profit margins are going to be too small, investors should rightly be concerned. One of Sam Walton's core principles when building the Walmart empire was to always control costs better than the competition. That's where he found his advantage, and sustainability. Not everyone wants to run a discount business, but there is no lack of scale or revenue at Walmart.

Buzzwords

Peter Thiel says that the use of buzzwords is one of his pet peeves and biggest turnoffs. Forget the jargon when speaking with investors. Deliver substance.

Founders Have Other Jobs

Is this just a hobby for the founder? A part-time gig? Or are founders really serious and dedicated to making this work? Are founders available enough, and at the right times, to make the venture work?

Founders Have No Other Source of Income

Don't expect investors to be throwing millions on the table for you to go off and buy a bigger house, get a new car, party half the week away, and generally upgrade your lifestyle. This is money to use to carefully and prudently grow the business. Investors may be split on whether it is better for startup founders to have another job or not, but those without another source of income or some financial reserves could be prone to making rash mistakes. Whatever your situation is, make sure that you can eloquently convey the pros and cons.

Poor Credit Ratings

You may have been beat into foreclosure and default on almost everything back around 2008, but what does your track record look like before and after that blip? If there are small charge-offs you can pay off, does it make sense to clear that up? Are you up to date on your taxes? Failing to pay taxes as a business and business owner can be catastrophic for everyone involved. If you are at risk of being hit with a federal tax lien, consider at least working out a payment agreement with the IRS.

Weak Marketing Plans

Scaling and generating real revenues is going to require a realistic and aggressive plan. If this isn't your area of expertise, look for guidance.

Relying Only on Paid Advertising

Building on the previous point; startups can't rely only on paid advertising. Especially if they have only identified one or two channels to use. There may be times when funds are tight, and you need to be able to generate sales regardless of fundraising success, and profits and profit margins will be a lot better if there are other sales channels working.

Blind Optimism

You have to be an optimist to launch a startup, but unrealistic, blind optimism isn't going to sell investors, and it isn't going to make for a sustainable startup. Be positive, but acknowledge the real challenges that exist too.

Claims of Having No Competition

Claiming you have no competition is a sign of being overly optimistic. There will be the potential for some form of competition. Recognize it, and admit it, and you'll gain credibility and investors will be confident that you are on top of it.

No Technical Founders

If you aren't technical, and you have no technical founders, that means there will likely be significant cost in paying for technical development and maintenance. That is a hard cost that the venture may not survive without. Contrast that setup with having at least two or three cofounders who cover all of the main functions and skill sets.

Asking for Too Much or Too Little Capital

This can be a red flag that founders may not really know that they are up against. Don't be too shy. Don't forget that you can raise additional capital in further rounds.

Poor Use of Previous Funds

Startups that have burned through previous rounds of funding without generating results can be a scary proposition. Note that this doesn't necessarily have to mean break even or, in some cases, revenues. Some of the biggest stories of recent years appear to have changed these rules. However, you've got to have something to show for it.

Early Investors Not Participating in Additional Funding Rounds

If previous investors are not getting in on a round, that can definitely be a bad sign. If there is a good reason for that, make sure to address it proactively, rather than allowing it to work against you.

Entrepreneurs Have No Financial Skin in the Game

When launching a startup, entrepreneurs know they are going to be putting in a lot of time and energy. But many have no financial skin in the game. It's not really about the amount, it is about equal risk sharing. You are probably looking for investors who will not just bring money, but will also put in some work. You want them to bring some effort, their contacts, their expertise, and a lot of money to the deal. From the other side of the table, it makes investors feel a lot better if founders are putting some money in, too.

Lack of Momentum

Even if you haven't raised any funds before, it is critical to track and show progress. It doesn't have to be huge. It can be revenue, users, market share, or another metric you are focusing on. But make sure you are tracking and reporting traction and momentum.

Moving the Ball Forward . . .

Being alert to these red flags, and tackling them in advance is smart when it comes to clearing the path to getting funded fast. To save precious time, be prepared, streamline the process, clear any potential hurdles, and find the most efficient method of raising capital.

Follow this formula to prevent fundraising from slowing your startup down at every stage. Then find the best channel for raising the capital your startup craves. When you do that, raising capital and completing successful rounds of funding can happen a lot faster than you thought.

Ultimately none of the red flags above are a show stopper. As a founder, what you need to do is put a correction wherever it needs to be placed to address potential concerns and have a good explanation behind it.

Fundraising is without a doubt an art. As you have read throughout this book there are many things that need to be aligned in order to close the financing and have it available in the bank. However, if you are able to nail it on the suggestions and tips provided here, you are well on your way to making it happen. Keep your head up, be patient, and never accept a no for an answer. You are the architect of your startup's future, and with hard work and dedication anything is possible.

Good luck!

Glossary

In this handy glossary of terms you'll find a list of key definitions that you should familiarize yourself with before and during your journey as a startup founder looking for investment.

angel investor: An investor primarily involved in early startup investment. (Often a one-off investment made by family or friends to help a startup founder get a project up and running, or a cash injection to help a business weather a difficult period.)

antidilution protection: A clause in a contract that protects some investors from their equity or shares' dilution when other investors buy stock in a company. This is often applied when shares in a company are sold at a value less than the amount paid originally by existing investors.

board of advisors: A group of individuals who offer advice to the management of a company. This is an informal relationship and not legally binding, but can provide valuable strategic policies.

board of directors: A group of individuals who are appointed to collectively appraise and oversee all company activities. This is a formal arrangement and therefore the mandates made by directors must be carried out.

business plan: A systematic breakdown of how a business will develop. This clearly states any expenses needed to achieve specific goals within a given timeframe.

Bonds: A form of debt investment. In this case an investor offers a loan to a business in return for bonds equaling that value. These can then be cashed in after an agreed-upon amount of time, and at a specified rate of interest. Bond owners are therefore creditors rather than shareholders and have no say over a company's strategies.

cap table: A capitalization table, displayed in table form; a breakdown of how much equity in a business is owned by relevant individuals or groups. This helps to clarify the percentage of ownership before and after an investment round, as well as any equity dilution and the current value of equity itself.

CEO: A chief executive officer. Responsible for all managerial decisions, and ultimately in charge of the business unless removed by a board of directors.

common stock: Represents company ownership. Shares allow their owners to vote on corporate policy and to have a say on serving directors. If liquidation or a sale should occur, common stock owners are paid an amount only after bond owners and preferred stockholders.

completion schedule: An agreed-upon timeframe for completing all administrative and procedural tasks in order to sign off on an investment.

corporate structure: A description of how each department (marketing, human resources, accounting, etc.) within a business contributes to the overall vision and goals of the organization.

crowdsourcing: Innovative, hassle-free way to seek investment by using third-party companies such as Onevest to match your startup with ideal investors.

equity: Security or stock that represents ownership in a business.

financial forecast: Also known as a financial projection, a forecast estimates growth and income for a business over a given time, based on comparison with existing businesses and market research.

IPO: Known as an initial public offering, an IPO is the first share offer made by a company to the public. This involves listing stock/shares on a stock exchange where the public can buy a portion of a company for an agreed-upon price. This price varies based on market forces on a daily basis.

liquidation preference: A clause in a contract that stipulates which investors receive payment first if a company is liquidated or sold, even before a company's founders in many cases. This is a common clause often used by venture capitalists to offset the risk of investment.

market research: A way to define consumer wants and needs. By carrying out market research studies, a startup can then streamline its approach to be more appealing to a target demographic.

market value: The amount an investor or consumer is willing to pay for something based on current consensus about how much a company, product, or service is actually worth.

outsourcing: Hiring a freelancer to complete a task for your business, rather than having you or your employees or a new hire do it. This is a common practice to reduce overhead and secure quality work without requiring full-time staff.

preferred stock: A form of share that has priority over common stocks. Preferred stock has a higher claim on assets and/or earnings, which often results in preference when any dividends are given out to shareholders: in other words, preferred stockholders get paid first. These dividends can be paid monthly or quarterly and share similar features with debt in that they can appreciate in price. Preferred stock usually comes with no voting rights, however.

prospect: Salesspeak for any customer or investor who fits a demographic. A person who is most likely to make an investment when approached. Also known as a potential investor.

seed funding: A model of funding where investors provide money to "seed" a business, giving it enough to operate for a short period of time. If it shows promise, subsequent investment may be offered.

series investment: A naming convention for investment rounds ("Series A," "Series B," etc.). Each round can fulfill a different function. Earlier rounds will be focused on establishing a company, while later rounds will revolve around expanding a company, brand, product, or service.

social media platform: Any website or app that allows users to communicate with each other and share their likes and dislikes. An essential marketing platform for businesses and a great way to engage with investors.

startup founder: Any individual who has created a startup business.

target demographics: A group of consumers that a startup founder wishes to market products/services to. This could be customers in an age group or living in a specific region, for example.

venture capitalist: An investor who supplies capital to small companies and startups in order to help them grow into profitable businesses. In some cases, this will be carried out as a venture capitalist fund (or group), in which many venture capitalists have collected their money together into a pool in order to reduce risk.

About the Author

Alejandro Cremades (alejandro@onevest.com, @acremades, www
.alejandrocremades.com) leads the vision and execution for Onevest
as its cofounder and executive chairman.

The Onevest ecosystem supports founders and investors in building successful ventures. Onevest provides technology products to
connect founders, investors, advisors, and influencers in the entrepreneurship community seamlessly and easily. Onevest is currently
operating 1000 Angels, the world's largest digital-first, invitation-only
investor network that allows members to build a venture portfolio free
of management fees, carried interest, or large capital commitments.

Members of 1000 Angels are provided with the ability to create
their own venture portfolios from a constantly updated selection of
high-quality, exclusive investment opportunities in some of the most
exciting high-growth, early-stage companies in the world. Member-
ship is open by invitation to accredited investors only.

In addition, Onevest is operating CoFoundersLab, which is the
leading matchmaking service for founders, connecting them with
other cofounders, advisers, and interns. CoFoundersLab has also
partnered with some of the major startup hubs, including universities

and accelerator programs, to assist them in fostering innovation and building teams that would later launch startups.

Prior to Onevest, Alejandro was an attorney at King & Spalding, where he was involved in one of the largest investment arbitration cases in history, with $113 billion at stake (*Chevron vs. Ecuador*).

Alejandro guest lectures at NYU Stern School of Business and the Wharton Business School, and has been included in the Top 30 under 30 lists of *Vanity Fair*, *Entrepreneur Magazine*, *and GQ Magazine*.

Alejandro has also been involved with the JOBS Act since inception. He was invited to the White House and the U.S. House of Representatives to provide his views on the new regulatory changes.

Index